MENTOR

HOW ALONG-THE-WAY DISCIPLESHIP WILL CHANGE YOUR LIFE

CHUCK LAWLESS

LifeWay Press®
Nashville, Tennessee

ISBN 978-1-4627-8790-6 • Item 005800753

Dewey decimal classification: 158
Subject headings: MENTORING \ CHRISTIAN LIFE \ BIBLE—BIOGRAPHY

Cover design: The Visual Republic

To order additional copies of this resource, write to LifeWay Resources Customer Service; One LifeWay Plaza; Nashville, TN 37234; fax 615-251-5933; phone toll free 800-458-2772; order online at LifeWay.com; email orderentry@lifeway.com; or visit the LifeWay Christian Store serving you.

Printed in the United States of America

Groups Ministry Publishing • LifeWay Resources • One LifeWay Plaza • Nashville, TN 37234

CONTENTS

ICON LEGEND

 Fun facts and useful
tidbits of information

 Things
to watch

 Expanding on
biblical concepts

 On the web

 Digging deeper into
study concepts

 Available tools for
group leaders

ABOUT THE AUTHOR
CHUCK LAWLESS

My name is Chuck. My wife, Pam, and I grew up in Ohio, but we live in Wake Forest, North Carolina. I serve at Southeastern Baptist Theological Seminary as the dean of doctoral studies and the vice president of spiritual formation. I'm also the team leader for theological-education strategists for the International Mission Board of the Southern Baptist Convention. Prior to these roles I pastored churches in Ohio and taught at the Southern Baptist Theological Seminary in Louisville, Kentucky. You may connect with me via my website at www.chucklawless.com.

Pam and I were introduced by two church secretaries, and we've been married for more than twenty-five years. For most of those years, I've served as a pastor and seminary professor. We've had the fun of hanging out with more than one generation of students, and I love seeing what God is doing now through men and women in whom we've invested. They're serving now as pastors, missionaries, church planters, and faithful lay leaders in churches around the world.

You'll read about some of these stories in this Bible study. You'll also hear about men who've poured their lives into me, helping me grow so that I can invest in others. Because I've gained so much through mentoring, I'm thrilled that you're taking time to complete this study. As you do, I pray that God will direct you to develop your own mentoring relationships.

WELCOME TO THE MENTOR PROCESS

WE WERE ON A RAFT HEADED DOWN THE OCOEE RIVER IN TENNESSEE. THE RAPIDS WERE ROUGH, AND THE WATER WAS SPEWING, BUT SELDOM HAD I HAD AS MUCH FUN. WHAT MADE THE TRIP FUN, THOUGH, WASN'T SO MUCH THE RAFTING BUT THE COMPANY I WAS WITH—BRANDON AND CHRIS, A COUPLE OF GUYS IN WHOM I HAD BEEN INVESTING MY LIFE. BOTH WERE STUDENTS WHERE I WAS TEACHING. ONE WAS PREPARING TO BE A PASTOR AND THE OTHER A MISSIONARY.

I had taken my first rafting trip the previous year with Brandon. He was a rafting veteran, and I was a rookie. He taught me strategies like how to read the rapids, how to row effectively, and how to lock in my feet when approaching the rapids. I may have been his mentor, but he was the teacher that day. And the waters became less a threat to me because I knew he was with me.

That's what this Bible study is about—people traveling through life together, navigating rough waters when necessary, and staying focused on the goal. It's about one person pouring his life into another person until the student becomes the teacher. And ultimately, it's about the mentor sending the mentee out so that he can guide others on their journey.

Welcome to this journey. We'll explore how to live our faith by purposefully walking through life together. The sessions in this study are based on Scripture, which is inspired by God (see 2 Timothy 3:16). They're also written with a certain audience in mind—Christians who are mentoring other Christians in the context of a local church or ministry.

Not only will we examine Jesus' practices in mentoring, but we'll also look at Paul's work of mentoring in the early church. In the New Testament Paul and Timothy are classic examples of a mentor and a mentee. Paul, an apostle, church leader, and missionary, mentored Timothy, a young minister and evangelist, who in turn then mentored others in the faith. All of us need to be both a Paul (a mentor) and a Timothy (a mentee). We need to be influenced and to influence others. I hope this study will help you become both. The road map for our walk together looks like this.

> Sometimes mentoring is messy, but the walk is worth the effort.

Session 1 describes the journey of a mentor: why that role exists and what it looks like. Sessions 2–3 focus on Jesus and Paul as examples of first-century mentors. Sessions 4–5 offer practical tools and strategies for mentoring and being mentored. Session 6 points out potholes and possibilities we could face as we journey through life together in faith.

Each session will take you into the Bible, challenge you to think about your life, and encourage you to invest in others. Reflection questions and application suggestions will encourage you to do more than simply read the words; the goal is for you to do something with what you learn. Each session also includes a general suggestion for those who are already in a mentoring relationship.

So let's press forward together. My prayer is that all of us will learn from one another along the way.

SESSION ONE

UNDERSTANDING ALONG-THE-WAY DISCIPLESHIP

My list of people who've invested in my life is a long one: Randy Richards, Glenn Davidson, Steve Bauer, Brother Jack Tichenor, Don Betts, Lawrence Langford, Sonney Allen, Ed Hensley, Big Dave Ensor, Ronnie Allen, Ralph Harvey, and Thom Rainer. Their roles are all different—pastors, deacons, laypersons, professors, fathers in the faith, father-in-law—but these men and others have changed my life. Some earned college, even seminary, degrees. Some taught me in Sunday School, and some taught me how to conduct Sunday School. Some would be surprised that they're even on my list, and that's one of the facts I love most about them.

These men have been mentors to me—disciplers, coaches, friends. I've had the privilege of walking in the shadows of some great men of God. Maybe you've had the same privilege. If not, perhaps completing this study will help you find a mentor or become one.

Who has invested in and influenced your life?

How would you describe their motivation for investing in you?

WHAT'S MENTORING ANYWAY? A SIMPLE DEFINITION
Here's my definition of *mentoring*. Mentoring is:

> A God-given relationship in which one growing Christian encourages and equips another believer to reach his or her potential as a disciple of Christ[1]

We'll explore this definition as we move through this session.

Mentoring is about relationships.

The Bible is filled with stories of people who invested in other people. Moses and Aaron. Moses and Joshua. Eli and Samuel. Naomi and Ruth. Elijah and Elisha. Jesus and the disciples. Paul and Timothy. Paul and Silas. Paul and Titus. Barnabas and John Mark. This list shouldn't surprise us, because God is a God of relationships.

This fact is obvious, not only from God's very nature as Father, Son, and Holy Spirit (see 2 Corinthians 13:13) but also from the creation account. God created human beings to be in relationship with Him and one another (see Genesis 2:8-25). When He chose to provide salvation, He did it personally by coming to earth, dying as the sacrifice in our place, and breaking the power of death (see Romans 5:12).

Now God has given us the church—that is, Christian people—to relate to us, teach us, and guide us. The church loves one another, serves one another, prays for one another, confronts one another, and forgives one another. This body of Christ, when obedient to its marching orders, produces disciples by preaching the gospel and teaching believers (see Matthew 28:18-20). When we develop discipling relationships, then, we're doing what God told us to do.

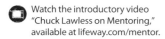 Watch the introductory video "Chuck Lawless on Mentoring," available at lifeway.com/mentor.

Mentors thrive in divine intersections.

I'm amazed by the way God orchestrates divine intersections in His church, crossroads in which we meet the people He has waiting for us. Brother Jack Tichenor was one divine intersection for me. In many ways Brother Jack was the mentor who guided me in most of the major decisions I made as a young pastor, although he never officially served as my pastor. I met him only after he retired from being a pastor and joined my home church, yet he quickly made time for another preacher boy. Many days I sat with him in his den (or in his garage watching his electric trains go by) as we talked about ministry. He was such a natural mentor that more than forty young men under his teaching entered the ministry during his sixty years of preaching.

One of those young men was Will. Will's family members had been longtime members of Brother Jack's church, and they also joined my home church after Jack retired. Will was four years younger than I, but we quickly connected. I became his Sunday School teacher, and he and I spent many hours together during our teen years. He later became my college roommate and led music at the first church I pastored. Almost two decades later I also served as his supervising professor in his doctoral work. Both unofficially and officially, I was blessed for years to mentor Will, who had first learned under Brother Jack, my mentor, long before I met either one of them.

Divine intersections. God is a specialist at creating them.

What divine intersections have you experienced?

Describe the person who's your Brother Jack.

Mentoring requires a growing Christian.

In a mentoring relationship one person leads, and another follows. Somebody must be in front, even if only slightly. Only when we're growing can we guide others toward growth.

Ideally, believers have both mentors who teach them and disciples they teach. We find an example in the New Testament in the relationship between Paul and Timothy. Paul was a leading apostle in the early New Testament church and the writer of multiple New

Testament letters. He served as a mentor to Timothy, a younger early-church leader. We all need a Paul and a Timothy. Our Paul challenges us to grow, and we then urge our Timothy to grow also. In this way mentoring becomes a generational effort as the person we mentor gleans not only from our influence but also from the influence of our mentors (and our mentor's mentor and so on).

My friend Tom may not think of himself as a Paul to me, but he has been in many ways. I first knew him from a distance as a great preacher and leader in my denomination, and I met him when his son became my student. Over the years I've watched him lead a church, retire from pastoral ministry, take on another denominational role, walk beside his first wife during a long bout with cancer, and pray that all of his grandchildren would become followers of Jesus.

Because I wasn't raised in a Christian home, I needed a role model like Tom to help me know how to love my wife and lead my home. I know the Bible tells me to love Pam as Christ loved the church (see Ephesians 5:25), but that doesn't mean I always fully understand how to do that. Men like Tom challenge me to improve as a husband.

Tom's first wife passed away, and he has now remarried. What amazed me most was that Tom first thought about remarrying when his mentor—then more than ninety years old—challenged him to consider that possibility. A ninety-year-old growing Christian pushed a seventy-year-old growing Christian to keep growing. That's what mentoring should look like.

A mentor has to keep growing spiritually, but mentors are seldom ahead of their disciples in every area of life. Everybody has strengths and weaknesses, and everybody has room for growth. Your mentor (or you as a mentor) might be strong in Bible study but weak in prayer. You may have more passion for personal evangelism than for social justice. A mentor who's single won't be as prepared to give marriage advice as one who's married.

Our goal as mentors is to teach from our strengths and keep working on our weaknesses so that we can continue to grow. That's another reason we need mentors. They point out our weaknesses, challenge us to admit our struggles, give us direction in dealing with those issues, rejoice with us when we experience victory, and love us anyway when we fail. Everybody benefits when our ever-growing mentors motivate us to keep moving forward.

Mentoring is a balance of encouraging and equipping.

Following Christ is difficult. A very real enemy fights against us (see Ephesians 6:11-12). Trials happen. Disappointments come. Friends sometimes reject our message or betray

 In Greek mythology the story of Mentor is found in Homer's famous work *The Odyssey*. When Odysseus, the king of Ithaca, went to war, he entrusted the care of his son, Telemachus, to a friend, Mentor. The name came to designate a wise teacher, guide, and counselor for another person.

us. Trusting God is difficult when life seems unfair or the future is unclear. Without encouragement, giving up is a real temptation. Mentors can help in times like these. Good mentors encourage us when we're stressed and equip us when we need training.

John is one of those encouragers in my life. Serving on the mission field for many years, he faced some of the most difficult situations I've ever heard of. Still I've watched him reach out to young pastors and missionaries, reminding them that God is bigger than anything they face and strengthening their faith with his presence. I've never been with him when he didn't say something to me like "I'm glad the Lord gave us this friendship." If you have somebody like John on your side, you'll press forward through tough times. That kind of encouragement can make a big difference.

Who encourages you like that? A parent? A teacher? Another believer?

We need more than encouragement, though. In the midst of life's struggles, we also need help doing what God calls us to do. We know we need to study the Bible, but we don't always know how. Pastors tell us that prayer matters, but we don't always understand how to pray. Telling others about Jesus is essential but not always modeled. We don't need someone to tell us what to do as much as we need someone to show us how to do it. We need equipping.

In addition to encouraging, mentoring teaches Christian disciplines and life skills. Encouragement without equipping might lead to restored hope, but seldom does it produce life transformation—the goal of mentoring. Mentoring should change the way we live.

When I first started mentoring many years ago, I assumed I would focus almost exclusively on teaching spiritual disciplines like Bible study, prayer, and fasting. Since then I've met young people who want to be equipped in many more areas. The list is extensive: understanding the opposite gender, relating to parents, budgeting, retirement planning, buying life insurance, understanding God's will, playing racquetball, grilling a steak, buying a house, writing a résumé, finding a church, dealing with a health crisis, overcoming temptation, raising kids, purchasing a car, painting a wall, and on and on. This type of life-on-life equipping reminds us that our faith affects every area of our lives.

From your experience have your fellow believers been better at encouraging you or equipping you? Explain.

Describe one area in which you need equipping.

Mentoring is about transformation.

The goal of Christian mentoring is that the mentor lives like Jesus, the disciple becomes more and more like Jesus, and both continue to lead others to do the same. It's hard to find a loftier goal than becoming like Jesus. Mentoring matters in an eternal way.

Later in this session (and in session 3 of this study) we'll focus on some of the apostle Paul's writing to Titus, one of Paul's disciples among the early church leaders (see 2 Corinthians 8:16-17,23). Titus was to challenge people to invest their lives in other believers, just as Paul had invested his life in Timothy, Titus, and others. Paul expected believers to fulfill this calling because he knew God's purpose for all believers:

> **Those he foreknew he also predestined to be conformed to the image of his Son, so that he would be the firstborn among many brothers and sisters (Romans 8:29).**

According to this verse, if you're a follower of Jesus, God is in the process of making you more like His Son. The word *conformed* speaks of God's changing us, remaking us so that our lives model Christ. Ultimately, God will completely change us in heaven, so we'll be like His Son. While we're here on earth, He moves us in that direction. We call this process *sanctification,* defined by one theologian as "a progressive work of God and man that makes us more and more free from sin and like Christ in our actual lives."[2] Letting go of sin and living more like Jesus are two critical elements in this transformation.

We know for certain that God alone gives us victory as He makes us like Christ, but we cooperate with Him in this process. There's footwork for us to do in daily turning away from sin, putting our faith in God, and putting on the character of His Son. These verses reveal the choices we need to make as God transforms us:

> **Put away all the following: anger, wrath, malice, slander, and filthy language from your mouth. Do not lie to one another, since you have put off the old self with its practices and have put on the new self. You are being renewed in knowledge according to the image of your Creator (Colossians 3:8-10).**

 Titus is one of three New Testament books (along with 1–2 Timothy) commonly known as the Pastoral Letters. These letters include instructions from Paul to his protégés in the faith as they worked to address specific issues in New Testament churches.

Since we also have such a large cloud of witnesses surrounding us, let us lay aside every hindrance and the sin that so easily ensnares us. Let us run with endurance the race that lies before us, keeping our eyes on Jesus, the source and perfecter of our faith. For the joy that lay before him, he endured the cross, despising the shame, and sat down at the right hand of the throne of God (Hebrews 12:1-2).

Ridding yourselves of all moral filth and the evil that is so prevalent, humbly receive the implanted word, which is able to save your souls. But be doers of the word and not hearers only, deceiving yourselves (James 1:21-22).

With your minds ready for action, be sober-minded and set your hope completely on the grace to be brought to you at the revelation of Jesus Christ (1 Peter 1:13).

How does our responsibility to do our part in spiritual growth fit into the concept of mentoring? It applies to both the mentors, who are responsible for their own spiritual footwork, and the people being mentored, who need to be encouraged in their spiritual footwork. Titus, the mentee, had the responsibility of walking in faith as these Scriptures describe, but Paul, his mentor, helped him figure out how to do that. Their mentoring relationship probably encouraged both of them in this effort.

Paul urged his disciples to follow his example and thereby follow Jesus (see 1 Corinthians 11:1). He expected the people he mentored to mature in Christ, and he modeled Christianity in front of them and alongside them as they aimed for spiritual growth. The believers Paul mentored were becoming more and more like Jesus in the process. This is the key to mentoring.

Think about the Great Commission in Matthew 28:18-20, in which Jesus tells us to make disciples. To be like Jesus is to be willing to reproduce ourselves in other disciples, release them to do God's work (whether as laypersons or pastors), and support them as they invest in others—just as Jesus did. This is a foundational truth: mentors who invest in others as Jesus did will produce other mentors, and lives will be transformed.

Whom do you know who's growing to be more and more like Jesus?

Who's more like Jesus because of spending time with you?

WHAT ABOUT MENTORING IN THE EARLY CHURCH? A BIBLICAL DESCRIPTION

Some people see mentoring as just hanging out together. There's a place in mentoring for just hanging out, but biblical mentoring is more intentional and focused than that. Read these directions for mentoring that Paul sent to Titus:

> **You are to proclaim things consistent with sound teaching. Older men are to be self-controlled, worthy of respect, sensible, and sound in faith, love, and endurance. In the same way, older women are to be reverent in behavior, not slanderers, not slaves to excessive drinking. They are to teach what is good, so that they may encourage the young women to love their husbands and to love their children, to be self-controlled, pure, workers at home, kind, and in submission to their husbands, so that God's word will not be slandered. In the same way, encourage the young men to be self-controlled in everything. Make yourself an example of good works with integrity and dignity in your teaching. Your message is to be sound beyond reproach, so that any opponent will be ashamed, because he doesn't have anything bad to say about us (Titus 2:1-8).**

Clearly, mentoring is more than just hanging out. It's about along-the-way life transformation that illustrates the gospel.

Mentoring crosses spiritual generations.

Titus was working with the Christians in Crete, a poorly organized congregation threatened by false teachers. One solution to the problems in Crete was for growing believers to ground younger believers in the Christian faith. Older men (most likely men who were old enough to have raised families of their own) were to model Christian living for others by being clearheaded, respectable, and sensible. Their lives were to be characterized by good judgment and Christian dignity, their faith grounded in true doctrine, their love for God and others genuine, and their patience under trial obvious. This passage suggests that the older men were to model their faith particularly for the younger men in the church.

Sonney Allen modeled his faith in this way for me. Sonney was a deacon in the first church in which I served as the pastor. I was young, in my early twenties, and Sonney was a more mature believer. He hadn't attended college or seminary, but he was fully educated in life. He taught me about remodeling a home, practicing evangelism, and loving all kinds of people. I watched him as he loved his wife and son with a deep,

 "Paul wrote multiple times commanding converts to, 'Be ye followers of me.' Their Bible first had legs."—Waylon Moore, mentoring expert (mentoring-disciples.org)

sacrificial love. More important, I knew he loved me regardless of whether I made bad or good decisions. As a young pastor, I needed that kind of support.

Sonney later developed multiple illnesses. His pain was great, yet I never heard him complain. He still laughed, worshiped, and shared the gospel even as he was dying. Just before he died, I was honored to dedicate my doctoral dissertation to him. That was the least I could do for a mentor who showed me how to live as a godly man should.

The passage in Titus also has direction for older women to mentor younger women. These older women (old enough to have raised their families) were to live lives of reverence, not gossiping or overindulging in wine. They were to teach "what is good" (v. 3), not by formal schooling but by informal life-on-life modeling. Specifically, they were responsible for training younger women how to live their Christian faith. They were to teach them to love their husbands and children, to be self-controlled and pure, to take care of their homes in kindness, and to graciously follow their husbands' direction. By living holy lives and teaching others to do the same, the older women would honor God's Word.

It might surprise us to read that the older women were instructed to teach younger women such basic Christian responsibilities. Keep in mind, though, that this was still a new faith with a lifestyle ethic that was counterpoint to the worldview of the day. Even loving children as gifts from God rather than merely as economic blessings (particularly sons) was a radically different mindset. Younger women needed older Christian women to show them the way.

I think about Carol as I write these words. She was the mother of two teenagers, but she also poured her life into a group of young women in her small group in our church. She was much more to them than just their teacher; she was their friend, their model, and their listening ear. She loved them in their struggles but then prodded them to leave the nest when they were ready to lead others. Her life conversations with them during the week were often as important to them as their Sunday-morning activities. Carol was for these young women their Titus 2 example, an older woman who crossed the generations to make disciples.

For men only: What older man has been most influential in your life? How would you describe his investment?

 The term *homemakers* in Titus 2:5 doesn't mean that woman can't work outside the home but that the home should be the central place of ministry for a wife and mother.

For women only: What older woman has been most influential in your life? What words would you use to describe her?

Mentoring is done by believers who are growing in spiritual maturity.

After addressing older men and women, Paul turned his attention to Titus. Even as a younger man, Titus was to model Christian faithfulness for other young men. This is because whatever his age, a man growing in his faith, like Titus, has something to invest in other young men. Titus could model basic holy living by doing good deeds, discerning right doctrine, and exhibiting dignity and seriousness. Titus's words, whether in formal teaching or informal conversation, were to be so biblically consistent that even his opponents would have no case against him.

Here we learn a simple truth about mentoring: while mentoring through spiritual generations—older to younger—is essential, it's not the only model for mentoring. You don't always have to be older than people to be their mentor. Even younger believers can be mentors as long as they're being discipled. Investing in others requires only that you're one step ahead in some area—that you've learned something you can give to others. Whatever your age, life experience and Christian growth make the most effective tools for mentors.

Mentoring requires self-control.

Notice the number of times in this passage Paul called believers to be self-controlled. The older men and women and the younger men and women were to show self-restraint and mature judgment. They were to maintain control of their passions, thoughts, and words. Apparently, this was a significant issue for the believers in Crete, perhaps because one heresy running through the group was the idea that Christians could live in whatever manner they wanted without regard for morality.

Exhibiting self-control in an out-of-control culture isn't easy. One way to learn that kind of maturity is by watching others and allowing them to train you, that is, through mentoring. It's one thing to listen to people tell us to be self-controlled; it's another matter to watch them maintain control when they're wrongly accused, unfairly treated, dealing with a disappointment, or making mistakes. A Titus 2 ministry looks like this: believers who've been there train others who haven't, so when they get there, they'll honor God through the way they live. The evidence of our faith is best seen in day-to-day living.

Review the characteristics Paul told Titus the believers must attain (self-controlled, levelheaded, worthy of respect, sensible, sound in faith, etc.). Which do you think are most difficult to achieve and why?

Why do you think Paul emphasized self-control within each age and gender group?

WHY DOES IT MATTER? REASONS FOR MENTORING

When I became a believer many years ago, church discipleship ministries were organized almost entirely through directed Bible studies in small groups. These studies are important in discipleship, but they're not enough. They miss the most obvious New Testament means of disciple making: one-on-one, face-to-face mentoring. There are many reasons we should still invest our time and ourselves in this basic relational model.

Mentoring is biblical.

Jesus produced disciples by first investing in a group of twelve men, then more deliberately in three of those men, and most likely more specifically in one of those men—Peter. Jesus called them to be with Him, taught them, empowered them, prayed in their presence, sent them out, challenged them, called them to account, and even prepared a meal for them. They in turn became leaders in the early church.

The apostle Paul followed Jesus' model by pouring his life into a few young men like Timothy. This young protégé watched Paul minister, walked in his shadow, rejoiced with him when lives were changed, and prayed for him when he was persecuted. What joy Paul must have felt in knowing that after he was gone, Timothy would carry on the work of the gospel.

If Jesus and Paul made disciples through this means, it's a good pattern for us to follow.

Mentoring reinforces the truth of the Word.

When we watch our mentors share their faith, we're more likely to share our own faith. Spouses with godly marriages give us the invaluable gift of seeing Christian homes in motion. Life becomes an effective classroom when we get to see in action what we

 For a glimpse into a mentoring relationship in action, watch video session 1, "Jason and Jordan's Story," available at lifeway.com/mentor.

hear in God's Word. Many of God's truths came to life for me in the context of watching somebody else, even when the relationship wasn't an official mentoring relationship.

I met Herbert when the church where he was a deacon called me as its pastor. I was very much a rookie pastor, and I worried about every decision I made. I preached God's promises without first trusting them myself. Herbert, though, had learned over the years to trust God fully. He believed it was foolish to worry, because God was in control. Through this humble, trusting man I was reminded that God always keeps His word.

Ruby played that same role for the young women in our church. She was energetic, friendly, exuberant, passionate—the kind of person who exudes the presence of Jesus. When she started praying, you could tell that she touched heaven with her serious, heartfelt praying. She taught us that fervent prayer from righteous people makes a difference.

Mentoring requires mentors to guard their lives against the enemy's attacks.

If you choose to be a Christian mentor, you'll wear a bull's-eye on your back for Satan's attacks. If he can seriously wound the mentor, those who follow will bear the scars of that fall. Never does a mentor fall without a ripple effect. Understanding that, if you choose to be a mentor, you must guard yourself.

Why do people in leadership, who have great influence over other people, often fall to the enemy's attacks? My friend J. D. Greear, a pastor in North Carolina, warns that living in isolation contributes to the moral failures plaguing our culture. God created us to be in relationship with Him and others, and anything less than that opens the door for Satan. Greear says:

> **God never intended any of us to live alone. Deep friendships with people you live and work and go to church with are a part of discipleship. The shepherd is still a sheep.**[3]

A shepherd fights the same battles that the sheep fight. This confirms what mentoring is: "a God-given relationship in which one growing Christian encourages and equips another believer to reach his or her potential as a disciple of Christ." Mentoring creates a positive cycle. Good mentors stand their ground against the enemy because they don't want to harm their witness before their mentees and the unbelieving world. And in the very practice of mentoring, they're keeping themselves in relationship with other growing Christians, thus reinforcing their ability to stand their ground.

Who's watching your life? Who would know if you fell?

What steps do you consider essential to guard your life against the enemy's attacks?

Mentoring relationships offer a safe place to deal with failure.

Other than mentoring relationships, believers have few people to hold them accountable in their faith walks. Mentors model holiness, call their disciples to the same, and hold them accountable to that standard.

What happens when disciples fail to meet that standard? In that case the mentor has the opportunity to model the kind of forgiveness, grace, and mercy that enable the people being mentored to correct their course and return to the fight. In mentoring relationships confession is essential. People must be utterly honest. Spiritual full disclosure brings our sin out of the enemy's darkness into God's light, where we can eradicate it through repentance and forgiveness.

Mentors who grant grace to people who've failed aren't ignoring or negating the consequences of sin. Instead, they're modeling God's love to fallen but repentant people. Good mentoring creates an atmosphere for honest confession because the mentee knows that admitting the truth won't result in less love or acceptance.

In this kind of relationship, spiritual growth occurs in two directions. The mentor strives for holiness out of obedience to God and love for the mentee, and the mentee chooses obedience out of gratitude to God for His mercy shown through the mentor. Paul described dealing with this kind of issue:

> **Brothers and sisters, if someone is overtaken in any wrongdoing, you who are spiritual, restore such a person with a gentle spirit, watching out for yourselves so that you also won't be tempted (Galatians 6:1).**

In effective mentoring, mentors pick up struggling disciples, always being careful to guard their own hearts. Safety in failure discourages future failure.

 We don't hear the word *mentee* often. Although it sounds like a marine animal, it's the term for a person in the process of being mentored or discipled. Some people use *mentoree*.

Mentoring produces the next generation of Christian leaders.

I keep in my files a Father's Day card from Brandon, my Ocoee River guide in whom I invested significant time. The message on the card is simple, but it reverberates like a megaphone to me: "Thanks for being a father in my life." That card encourages me to press on when I get tired of the bureaucracy, paperwork, meetings, and tedious tasks that sometimes accompany a seminary administrative job. This kind of divine intersection is one of the greatest benefits of mentoring.

Mentoring is costly. We have to prioritize; spending time with others usually means deleting something else from the calendar. We have to be vulnerable; our own sins are magnified when others are watching. We often have to spend money; the costs of study resources, shared meals, and occasional travel expenses quickly add up. We may be misunderstood; mentors sometimes get accused of having favorites. And too often we experience disappointment; mentees sometimes fail. There are times when a mentor might wonder whether mentoring is worth the effort.

Being mentored is also risky. Your mentor might disappoint you. You might expect more than he or she can give. The time required usually means you have to give up something else. The push to live a holy life and maintain accountability might make you uncomfortable. You may be less willing to invest in somebody else in turn.

On the other hand, the risks you take as you're mentored might result in the amazing gift of a person in your life. God might give you a mentor and friend whose faith challenges you to greater faithfulness. The risks you take as you mentor others may breed disciples whose faith is potent and whose progress is obvious. You may grow spiritually as never before, and you might watch God use the people you've discipled in ways you had never dreamed. You might receive a father, son, mother, or daughter in the faith.

I'll take that risk any day.

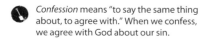 *Confession* means "to say the same thing about, to agree with." When we confess, we agree with God about our sin.

THROUGH THE WEEK

> **CONNECT:** Make a list of people who've been Pauls for you. Make a phone call, send an email or text, or write a letter to say thanks. Let them know what you've gained by walking through life with them.

> **PRAY:** If you don't currently have a mentor, begin asking God to provide one.

> **OBSERVE:** Watch for divine intersections in your life this week.

> **A SUGGESTION FOR MENTORS:** Make sure your mentees know the full story of your Christian journey. Take time to tell them about your ups and downs, victories and defeats, questions and answers. Invite them to ask questions about your journey.

> **A SUGGESTION FOR MENTEES:** Whenever God teaches you something, be sure to tell someone else what you've learned. Get in the habit of sharing what you're discovering along the way, and God might provide someone you can invest in.

1. Chuck Lawless, *Making Disciples through Mentoring* (Forest, VA, and Elkton, MD: Church Growth Institute, 2002), 14.
2. Wayne Grudem, *Systematic Theology* (Grand Rapids, MI: Zondervan, 1994), 746.
3. J. D. Greear, "Why Pastors Fall into Moral Sin," September 30, 2010, www.jdgreear.com.

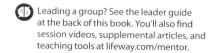 Leading a group? See the leader guide at the back of this book. You'll also find session videos, supplemental articles, and teaching tools at lifeway.com/mentor.

SESSION TWO

LEARNING FROM THE MASTER: JESUS & HIS DISCIPLES

What was the first Christian book you read? One of the first ones I read was a classic called *In His Steps* by Charles M. Sheldon.[1] I read it because my friend Will's parents recommended it to me (recommending spiritual-growth resources is something else older Christians can do for younger Christians).

In His Steps asks a critical question in its subtitle: "What would Jesus do?" It tells the story of a fictional congregation whose members committed to living their lives for one year by first asking this question. Needless to say, that commitment changes their lives.

Centuries later we're asking that same question in this session about Jesus and mentoring. The good news is that the Bible answers the question for us in the Books of Matthew, Mark, Luke, and John by describing Jesus' mentoring relationship with His disciples.

MAKING DISCIPLES: JESUS' COMMAND

Not long before the resurrected Jesus returned to His Father, He met His followers on a mountainside in Galilee. There He gave them these marching orders:

> **Jesus came near and said to them, "All authority has been given to me in heaven and on earth. Go, therefore, and make disciples of all nations, baptizing them in the name of the Father and of the Son and of the Holy Spirit, teaching them to observe everything I have commanded you. And remember, I am with you always, to the end of the age" (Matthew 28:18-20).**

The Great Commission is familiar to anyone who's spent much time in a Bible-teaching church. Sometimes we hear the word *go* as the command in this text, but the clearest command in the original Greek language of the New Testament is "make disciples" (v. 19). Making disciples isn't optional for followers of Jesus.

If making disciples is imperative, we must understand what the phrase actually means. It's a two-sided coin. On one side is an invitation to enter a relationship with the Master, Jesus, and to follow His teachings. This step is what we call conversion, when we turn from our sin and trust Christ for salvation. That conversion is publicly illustrated by the act of baptism.

On the other side of the coin is a call to Christian growth through obeying (or observing; see verse 20) everything Jesus commanded us to do. We call this process "discipleship." Those who choose to walk in Jesus' path will know and follow His teachings—including His order to teach others His commands. Therefore, making disciples should result in more disciples, who make even more disciples.

Here's the way one scholar described this two-sided coin of discipleship:

> **If those outside of the faith are not hearing the gospel and being challenged to make a decision for Christ, then the church has disobeyed one part of Jesus' commission. If new converts are not faithfully and lovingly nurtured in the whole counsel of God's revelation, then the church has disobeyed the other part.[2]**

"The other part" is the focus here. How will new believers know Jesus' teachings? How will they learn about Christian standards for relationships, morality, and giving? How will they know what Jesus expects? There's only one answer: someone must

 Charles Sheldon was the author of *In His Steps,* the fictional story of a church challenged to ask, "What would Jesus do?" before doing anything. Though the book was published in 1896, its question still dominates Christian thought.

teach them. We can't expect untaught believers to obey commands they don't know. Mentors who make disciples are necessary in the church, and equally important are believers who desire to be mentored in their walks with Jesus. Genuine believers, in fact, should want to be mentored.

Think about the churches you've attended. Were most better at evangelizing or discipling?

Why do you think Jesus started the Great Commission with "All authority has been given to Me" (v. 18)?

Making disciples through mentoring is personal.

Matthew 28:18-20 is probably the best-known expression of the Great Commission, but four additional similar texts are found in the New Testament:

> He said to them, "Go into all the world and preach the gospel to all creation" (Mark 16:15).

> He opened their minds to understand the Scriptures. He also said to them, "This is what is written: The Messiah would suffer and rise from the dead the third day, and repentance for forgiveness of sins would be proclaimed in his name to all the nations, beginning at Jerusalem. You are witnesses of these things" (Luke 24:45-48).

> Jesus said to them again, "Peace to you. As the Father has sent me, I also send you" (John 20:21).

> You will be my witnesses in Jerusalem, in all Judea and Samaria, and to the end of the earth (Acts 1:8).

Some writers believe more than Jesus' eleven remaining disciples heard Him speak the Great Commission (perhaps as many as five hundred people; see 1 Corinthians 15:6). That's possible, but the number of hearers isn't the point. The point is that Jesus' words were meant personally for every believer. As the Father sent Him, Jesus in His

 The word translated *disciple* means "a learner, one who follows a teaching." This term occurs approximately 250 times in the New Testament as either *disciple* or *disciples*.

authority sends His followers to proclaim the Word and to make disciples. Each of us must practice evangelism and mentor the people who come to faith in Jesus.

What are you doing to fulfill the Great Commission? If you aren't doing anything, have a conversation with someone who can help you figure out how to begin— perhaps your small-group leader or pastor.

Making disciples through mentoring is global.

Although the word *go* isn't a command in the original text of Matthew 28:19 in the same way it's translated in English, that's not to say the Great Commission doesn't require us to make disciples of people around the world. In fact, four of the five Great Commission passages in the New Testament clearly speak of the nations or the world. It's our responsibility to make disciples of all *nations,* a word that most likely refers to ethnic people groups rather than geopolitical countries.

What does this command mean to you? It might mean God wants you to mentor internationals in your community who follow Jesus. God may bring a foreign-exchange student, an immigrant, or even a refugee believer from thousands of miles away to create a divine intersection with you. He might want you to learn to teach English as a second language so that you can develop relationships with other people groups. Or He could point you to your neighbors who've moved to your community from another part of the world. Don't miss these opportunities to obey Jesus' Great Commission command.

How many internationals do you cross paths with during your week?

What challenges could arise in mentoring someone from a different culture?

On the other hand, the global nature of mentoring might mean God has a mentor for you from a different ethnic group. You may find believers from other countries who've had significant gospel training. Occasionally, someone from a different cultural perspective can challenge your faith to a level of discomfort and subsequent growth.

Maybe you've taken a mission trip to a place where other believers taught you. I've traveled a lot, and I could write a book about truths others have taught me. Russian believers showed me how to pray, even though I was there to lead a prayer conference. Africans taught me to trust that God's power is greater than the power of any false gods or demons. South Asians illustrated for me a faith that rejoices even in suffering. East Asian believers who wept over their one copy of the Bible reminded me how blessed I am with my many copies of God's Word. None of these believers were official mentors, but they taught me nonetheless. As a result, I've made myself open to learning from internationals who live around me.

MAKING DISCIPLES: JESUS' METHOD

Jesus told His disciples to make disciples, and He modeled for them how to do that. Let's look at the way Jesus mentored His disciples and learn from His approach.

Jesus called His disciples in the context of relationships.

Jesus' approach to mentoring was a process, especially as He called His twelve disciples. Contrary to what we sometimes think, Jesus called these men in stages. As you read about these stages, think about people in your life who are in various stages of a relationship with you. Some may be only acquaintances. Others may be long-term friends. All who are Christians may be candidates for a mentor or mentee.

Stage 1: The Call to Come and See

The Gospel of John tells us that Jesus met some of His future disciples when John the Baptist first pointed Him out to them:

> The next day, John was standing with two of his disciples. When he saw Jesus passing by, he said, "Look, the Lamb of God!" The two disciples heard him say this and followed Jesus. When Jesus turned and noticed them following him, he asked them, "What are you looking for?" They said to him, "Rabbi" (which means "Teacher"), "where are you staying?" "Come and you'll see," he replied. So they went and saw where he was staying, and they stayed with him that day. It was about four in the afternoon (John 1:35-39).

John the Baptist, the forerunner of Jesus, knew his calling was to point others to Jesus (that's our calling too). Two of his disciples, Andrew and likely John the son of Zebedee, followed his direction by pursuing Jesus. John's enthusiasm about Christ was so great that his disciples left him behind and followed Christ, seeking a personal conversation with Him. Jesus saw them following Him and spent the day with them. "Come and you'll see" (v. 39), He said to them.

You too can be sensitive to what's happening spiritually in the lives of people around you. You can learn from other believers who are obviously growing in their walks with Jesus. Someone else may be battling the enemy, and you could help. Maybe a new believer is excited but confused about the next steps to take in his or her faith. Raise your spiritual antenna and watch for opportunities in the relationships God gives you. Invite others to come and see what it means to follow Jesus.

Whose spiritual life is so attractive to you that you would want that person to be your mentor?

Whose life are you already observing? Who's the person you need to invite to come and see what following Jesus means?

Stage 2: The Call to Give Up All

The story with John the Baptist is the first recorded encounter between Jesus and five of His potential disciples. He was their teacher, and they trusted Him. But they hadn't yet walked away from their regular jobs. That step didn't happen until Jesus called them to leave all behind to follow Him and become "fishers of men" (Mark 1:16-20). In response to that call, they left everything and followed Him.

In mentoring our role isn't to call every person to give up his or her job; God doesn't call everyone to full-time ministry. However, He demands first place in our lives. The first commandment makes that clear: anything that keeps us from wholeheartedly serving God is an idol that must be forsaken (see Exodus 20:3). In the mentoring process we're called to make God the priority of our lives and to lead others to do the same.

Stage 3: The Call to Apostle

In the last stage of the disciples' calling, Jesus chose twelve men to be *apostles,* a word that means "ones sent with a message." These were the disciples Jesus would most closely mentor:

 Researchers tell us there are sixteen-thousand-plus people groups around the world. Of these more than six thousand are considered unreached or least reached with the gospel. Visit joshuaproject.net for more information.

> **During those days he went out to the mountain to pray and spent all night in prayer to God. When daylight came, he summoned his disciples, and he chose twelve of them, whom he also named apostles (Luke 6:12-13).**

We can learn a lot from Jesus' choosing the Twelve.

1. *Jesus prayed—all night long, in fact.* From His larger group of followers, Jesus then selected His mentees. Prayer is an important part of the mentoring process because we want to invest in the people God selects for us. He might direct us in prayer to people who surprise us—mentees we had never considered.
2. *Jesus initiated the relationship.* He didn't wait for mentees to come to Him. He intentionally sought the men who would walk most closely with Him.
3. *Jesus selected ordinary men.* They weren't religious leaders or trained teachers. Rather, they were uneducated and unknown.
4. *Jesus called His disciples for a purpose.* He would send them out, and they would carry His message throughout the Roman Empire. Mentoring would result in ministry and mission.

How would you feel if someone asked to be your mentor?

How would you approach someone if you wanted to be his or her mentor?

Jesus spent time with His disciples.

The Gospel of Mark is the shortest of the four Gospels. It's action-packed, with fewer extensive teaching segments than the other Gospels. A quick look at Mark's record shows that Jesus shared life with His disciples. They watched Him heal the sick, exorcise demons, confront religious leaders, calm storms, raise the dead, walk on water, multiply food, and overturn tables. These men heard Him answer questions, preach to crowds, silence demons, speak parables, and pray to the Father. They ate with Him, discussed truth with Him, and ministered alongside Him.

All that was possible because Jesus spent quality time with His disciples. Indeed, He called them first to be with Him (see Mark 3:14), and their time with Him changed their world. Mentoring means we give a mentee much more than a book or a Bible study; we give ourselves to another person for the sake of the gospel.

 Mark, the Gospel writer, wasn't one of Jesus' disciples. It's likely that Simon Peter was the human source for the accounts in Mark's Gospel.

When I teach mentoring conferences, I always ask this question: "What do you think keeps people from entering a mentoring relationship, either as mentor or a mentee?" The answers vary. Fear of vulnerability often hinders the potential mentor. An unwillingness to commit to meetings gets in the way of possible mentees. Both groups are often unclear about the details of mentoring, especially if they've never been in a mentoring relationship. Overwhelmingly, though, the biggest perceived hindrance to mentoring is a lack of time.

Jesus and His disciples dealt with that objection. He simply made the time to be with them, and they prioritized their commitment to be with Him. That's the way mentoring should work.

Jesus gave tasks to His disciples and held them accountable.

Imagine following Jesus to the top of a mountain, where His garments are changed to a brilliant white. Then think about bowing in amazement when Moses and Elijah show up—the lawgiver and the prophet of Old Testament history who've been deceased for centuries:

> About eight days after this conversation, he took along Peter, John, and James and went up on the mountain to pray. As he was praying, the appearance of his face changed, and his clothes became dazzling white. Suddenly, two men were talking with him—Moses and Elijah. They appeared in glory and were speaking of his departure, which he was about to accomplish in Jerusalem. Peter and those with him were in a deep sleep, and when they became fully awake, they saw his glory and the two men who were standing with him. As the two men were departing from him, Peter said to Jesus, "Master, it's good for us to be here. Let us set up three shelters: one for you, one for Moses, and one for Elijah"—not knowing what he was saying. While he was saying this, a cloud appeared and overshadowed them. They became afraid as they entered the cloud. Then a voice came from the cloud, saying: "This is my Son, the Chosen One; listen to him!" (Luke 9:28-35).

Imagine God's voice saying, "This is my Son … ; listen to Him!" (v. 35). It's no wonder Simon Peter stated the obvious: "It's good for us to be here" (v. 33). Who would have known what to say in the midst of such a miraculous series of events? How would you have responded?

Peter didn't want to leave; instead, he wanted to build a tabernacle to mark this place. But Jesus wouldn't allow His disciples to stay on that mountain. There was still work for Him to do. There was still work for the disciples to do too—following in obedience, sharing the good news, and making more disciples. More immediately, a young boy possessed with a demon needed Jesus' help. For that reason Jesus went with His disciples back down the mountain to do His work. Good mentoring should always lead to godly action.

Jesus taught His mentees and expected them to act on His teachings. Luke 9–10 describes this sending process, including Jesus' instructions (see 9:1-6; 10:1-11). He sent them out to take on demons. He challenged them to figure out a way to feed more than five thousand people when they had far too little food. He required them to pray for more laborers even while they went out to preach and heal in His name.

When they returned, they gave Jesus a report of their travels. When they rejoiced in their spiritual power rather than in God's grace, He loved them enough to correct them, telling them not to be excited about their power over demons but about the fact that God accepted them and gave them life (see Luke 10:18-20). These interactions between Jesus and His apostles show us that accountability is a part of Christlike mentoring. Jesus had expectations for those who followed Him. He didn't love them less when those expectations weren't met, but He always called His followers to grow. We should do the same with the people we disciple.

Jesus gave His life for His disciples.

Jesus' death is central to our Christian faith. Apart from Jesus' shedding His blood for us, we can't be saved (see Hebrews 9:22). Jesus' cross shows how much He loved His disciples—and how much He loves us.

We don't ordinarily give our lives for the people we mentor in this same way. But we can love in such a way that we're willing to give our lives for them.

Tony Dungy served for six years as the coach of the Super Bowl-winning Indianapolis Colts. One of his heroes was John Thompson, the coach of the Georgetown University Hoyas. When Coach Thompson heard that a notorious drug dealer was influencing his Georgetown players, he personally and directly confronted the dealer. Listen to Dungy's reflections on that risky action:

> I immediately thought of Jesus' parable of the sheep and the shepherd in the Gospel of John, chapter 10. There, Jesus speaks of the difference between a hired hand and a shepherd. When a wolf comes and threatens the flock, the hired hand runs away, leaving the sheep—someone else's sheep—to fend for themselves. The shepherd, on the other hand, rises to the defense of his

 For a glimpse into a mentoring relationship in action, watch video session 2, "Leigh Ann and Heather's Story," available at lifeway.com/mentor.

sheep. He will *die* for the sheep, if necessary, because they are *his*. … I had to take a look in the mirror to determine whether I was exhibiting this relational quality: I cared about those I was leading, but was I willing to die for them if that became necessary for their well-being? I hoped the answer was yes, but I wasn't sure that it was—yet.[3]

That's doing for a mentee what Jesus would do—giving up your life. Imagine being one of the players that coach was protecting. It's easier to follow someone's leadership when you know that person is staking his or her life on you.

We don't often get such a dramatic opportunity to show people their value to us, but there are many ways, in Christ's name, we can give up our lives for those who follow us, such as the choices we make to be the kind of person they need to follow, the time we give them, and the opportunities we turn down. These are godly sacrifices, made as we invest ourselves in others to help them become more like Jesus.

Think of a person you know you're important to. How does the value that person places on you affect the way you listen to him or her?

Describe a time when someone sacrificed for you.

MAKING DISCIPLES: JESUS' POWER AND PRESENCE

Do you remember how many expressions of the Great Commission are found in the New Testament? There are five: Matthew 28; Mark 16; Luke 24; John 20; and Acts 1. In each of these Bible passages, Jesus sent the church to all people groups to tell the gospel and make disciples. Most of these passages also include His promise of power within His promise of presence:

> **Remember, I am with you always, to the end of the age (Matthew 28:20).**

> **Look, I am sending you what my Father promised. As for you, stay in the city until you are empowered from on high (Luke 24:49).**

> **After saying this, he breathed on them and said, "Receive the Holy Spirit" (John 20:22).**

> **You will receive power when the Holy Spirit has come on you (Acts 1:8).**

Jesus, in His authority as the Son of God, ordered us to make disciples by sharing the gospel and teaching believers. Then He assured us of the power to get the job done. The Father promised to empower us, the Son is always with us, and the Holy Spirit has come on us. What else do we need?

The Holy Spirit empowers us to teach the Word of God boldly and powerfully (see Acts 4:8,31). He produces the fruit of the Spirit in us (see Galatians 5:22-23) and gives us spiritual gifts to use in ministry (see 1 Corinthians 12:11). When we seek truth, the Spirit guides us (see John 14:17; 15:26). When we don't know how to pray, He intercedes for us (see Romans 8:26-27). The Spirit of God lives in us, and He gives us what we need to be growing mentors and mentees. We don't mentor in and from our own strength. We don't have to worry or wonder whether we'll know what to say at the right time or how to deal with every situation. We can simply walk through life with those we mentor, knowing God's presence and power are waiting at every turn.

Jesus' Power in Modern Mentors

I wish you could know people I've known who walk in the power of God, like my friend Christie. She became a Christian at a young age, but it wasn't until her adult years that she began to grow as a disciple. Always trusting God with a childlike faith, she became a crisis mentor for many young women who turned to her when perceived emergencies stole their peace. Christie was the mentor, but the Holy Spirit was really her power and peace.

I wish I could introduce you to Mike. He's one of guys I mentor, even though we're geographically separated by miles. As a student minister, he's committed to pouring his life into young men. What I love about Mike is that he first wants to grow himself, learning every day to lean more on God for his strength as he gives himself to others.

And I wish you knew Shirley, an older lady who has spent much of her life mentoring other women. She and her husband have lived in many places around the world, and she always found someone to invest in wherever they lived. When you walk in the power of the Spirit, He leads you to mentees and gives you wisdom to mentor.

How do we tap into this power that's promised in Scripture so that it's evident in our mentoring relationships? First, we admit we can't make disciples on our own. None of us can live holy lives in our own strength, and none of us can change somebody else's life. We all default toward pride, not humility. We're self-absorbed by nature, and that trait makes us less-than-ideal mentors or mentees. Let's just admit together that we can't do well in a mentoring relationship apart from God's power.

After admitting we can't do this on our own, we trust God for His power. To know God and recognize His authority are to understand that we live victoriously only through Him. Think about it. God is the warrior who led His people through the Red Sea (see Exodus 15:3). David fought the Philistine giant, not with a sword and a javelin but in the name of the Lord whose battle it was (see 1 Samuel 17:45-47). Jehaziel likewise assured Jehoshaphat of God's presence in the midst of battle with these words: "This is what the LORD says: 'Do not be afraid or discouraged because of this vast number, for the battle is not yours, but God's' " (2 Chronicles 20:15). We are to put on God's armor, not ours (see Ephesians 6:11).

Finally, we pray, following the lead of men and women of faith. Abraham, Moses, Nehemiah, David, Jeremiah, Daniel, and others prayed. Hannah and Mary prayed. Jesus prayed in the morning, into the evening, and through the night. He prayed passionately for His followers and for those who would follow them. The disciples asked for lessons on prayer. Peter and Paul prayed. When we admit our need for God, trust His power, and connect with Him through prayer, we tap into His power to form strong mentoring relationships.

Jesus' Power at Work

Imagine a blank sheet of paper in front of you. On that paper in your mind, list all the reasons you can think of to keep you from mentoring someone else. Your list might look like this: too little time, don't know enough, afraid of vulnerability, don't know where to start, not sure who the mentee would be, never mentored before, and so on.

Then make a separate list of reasons for not being mentored. Your list might overlap with the first one, but it will probably include other reasons too: not sure what being mentored would involve, not enough time, afraid of being vulnerable, unwilling to be accountable, not sure anyone would want to invest in me.

Finally, take a separate sheet of paper and write, "The Power and Presence of God." In your mind lay that second sheet across the first one, completely covering your excuses with the power of God. Let the final image sink in for a few minutes.

The picture in your mind should be clear. Jesus commanded us to make disciples, and He empowers us to obey His command. That combination means we have no excuse not to make disciples through mentoring. We must practice along-the-way discipleship.

What reasons would you give for not being in a mentoring relationship?

What reason to be a mentor can you imagine that's greater than all the reasons not to?

MAKING DISCIPLES: JESUS' PATIENCE

I love mentoring. I look forward to hanging out with the guys I teach and from whom I learn. Whatever I'm facing in life, mentoring encounters help me regain my focus on the importance of people. That doesn't mean, though, that I never need patience in dealing with the men I mentor. Sometimes I'm ready to toss in the towel.

That's when I'm glad to have Jesus' example to follow. Jesus' mentees were sometimes quite a challenge. The Gospel of Mark gives us some excellent examples:

• Sometimes the disciples struggled to realize who their mentor was. For instance, when He calmed the sea, they asked, "Who then is this?" (4:41).
• They didn't always understand what Jesus could do. They were "utterly astounded" (5:42) when He not only healed but also brought back to life the synagogue leader's twelve-year-old daughter.
• They failed to learn from previous miracles. In the Mark 8 account of the feeding of the four thousand, the disciples seemed to have no frame of reference for the way Jesus might feed the crowds, although they had already witnessed the feeding of the five thousand recorded in Mark 6.
• These mentees had God's power at their disposal, but they still failed in at least one exorcism, primarily because they lacked faith and prayer (see 9:14-29).
• These same disciples criticized others who defeated demons and even argued about which disciple was the greatest in the kingdom (see 9:33-41).
• They rebuked people for bringing children to their mentor (see 10:13-16).
• Two of the men dared to ask for the best seats in Jesus' kingdom (see 10:35-41).
• One of them betrayed Jesus to death (see 14:43-46).
• All of the disciples deserted Jesus when He was arrested (see 14:50).
• One of them denied being a mentee at all (see 14:66-72)

Is this the bunch you would pick as mentees? Jesus did. Jesus chose these men because He knew what the Father could do through them. He saw in them their potential for leadership in God's kingdom. To put it simply, Jesus called these men to Himself and patiently taught them, believing in faith that the Father was going to mold them to be what He wanted them to be. He chose men who were unknown and untrained. It's obvious that only by God's power would these men make a difference. That's part of the fun of mentoring—watching God take people who are powerless and give them power to do mighty things in His name.

 One of Jesus' mentees, Judas, was a traitor who never truly turned to Jesus as his Savior. Instead, he became a tool in God's hand to bring about Jesus' necessary death.

Robert Coleman is the author of *The Master Plan of Evangelism,* a study of Jesus' work with His disciples.[4] This book, one of the best-selling books ever written about evangelism, is about discipleship as much as evangelism. Jesus mentored His disciples so that they would be great evangelists.

What I respect so much about Dr. Coleman is that he lives what he wrote in his book. One of my former colleagues, Tim Beougher, was one of Coleman's mentees years ago. Around the world are other Christian leaders who studied in Dr. Coleman's shadow. In fact, he recently told me about the young men he will be talking on trips in the next several months—and he's more than eighty years old! To be honest, I wouldn't mind having the opportunity to walk in Dr. Coleman's shadow and learn from his experiences.

Jesus' work with His disciples reminds us that everybody can benefit from mentoring. If you sometimes get prideful, you're like James and John. If you speak too quickly at times, you're similar to Peter. If you forget God's miracles and take His presence for granted, you could have joined Jesus' disciples. If your faith occasionally wavers, you're one of the crowd. But there's good news: it's possible that God has planned a divine intersection for you to grow in His grace. God might be sending you the gift of a person to disciple you along the way.

If you want to be a mentor, don't miss Jesus' example of patience and persistence. Mentoring can be messy, time-consuming, and frustrating, especially if God directs you to mentor someone who has much room for growth. Giving up may seem a lot easier than pressing on. But don't give up. It's God's responsibility to empower and grow the people you mentor. At the end of the day, you're responsible to remain faithful to your task and to do what Jesus did.

 "[Mentoring] will be slow, tedious, painful, and probably unnoticed by people at first, but the end result will be glorious, even if we don't live to see it."—Robert Coleman, *The Master Plan of Evangelism*[4]

THROUGH THE WEEK

> CONNECT: The earlier a person has a mentor, the better. Find out about opportunities to invest in the life of a child in your community who may not have a mentor. Check with your local Big Brothers, Big Sisters, Boys & Girls Club, or the local school district.

> PRAY: If you aren't mentoring someone, ask God to direct you to a potential mentee. Also ask God to remind you of the patience He has shown you so that you can show patience to others.

> READ: Want to learn about famous disciple makers? Check out these biographies:

• John Wesley, http://www.ccel.org/ccel/wesley/journal
• Henrietta Mears, http://www.wheaton.edu/ISAE/Hall-of-Biography/Henrietta-Mears
• Dawson Trotman, discipleshiplibrary.com
• Bill Bright, http://www.wheaton.edu/ISAE/Hall-of-Biography/Bill-Bright
• Max Barnett, discipleshiplibrary.com

> A SUGGESTION FOR MENTORS: Prayer is a critical part of mentoring. Thankfully, the Bible gives us many examples of people talking to God. Read these passages during your quiet time:

• Abraham, Genesis 18	• Moses, Exodus 32–33
• Hannah, 1 Samuel 2	• Nehemiah, Nehemiah 1
• David, Psalm 51	• Jeremiah, Jeremiah 1
• Daniel, Daniel 6	• Jesus, John 17
• Peter, Acts 10; 16	

> A SUGGESTION FOR MENTEES: Read the accounts from the Gospel of Mark listed in the section "Making Disciples: Jesus' Patience." Talk to your mentor about what you learned and use these stories to encourage other believers as well.

---

1. Charles M. Sheldon, *In His Steps: What Would Jesus Do?* (Grand Rapids, MI: Revell, 1985).
2. Craig L. Blomberg, *Matthew,* vol. 22, New American Commentary, (Nashville: Broadman, 1992), 433.
3. Tony Dungy, *The Mentor Leader* (Carol Stream, IL: Tyndale, 2010), 93–94.
4. Robert Coleman, *The Master Plan of Evangelism* (Grand Rapids, MI: Revell, 1993).

SESSION THREE

MENTORING IN ACTION : PAUL & TIMOTHY

Sometimes you hear a story you simply must retell. Every time you tell it, your heart skips a beat or your skin tingles with chills. No matter how many times you repeat it, it still grabs you. This is one of those stories.

I knew what mentoring was, or at least I thought I did, but I hadn't thought much about the potential cost of investing in another person's life until I heard this man's story. I wasn't prepared for what the speaker said about mentoring. His passion inspired me, although I had heard most of the material before—until he spoke more personally about one of his mentors.

Here's my best memory of what he said: "The doctors discovered I needed a kidney. My mentor was a match, and he provided that kidney. Both of us entered the hospital, and one of his kidneys became mine. When I talk about my mentor investing in me, I really mean he's in me."

Maybe you now see why that moment took my breath away. Sometimes, apparently, mentoring costs you part of yourself.

In this session we'll study the mentoring ministry of the apostle Paul and the way he gave himself to this work. To get ready for that study, consider what you would include if you were writing a job description for the position of mentor. What would the background requirements be? College educated? Married? Single? A teacher? Trustworthy? Successful?

What qualities would you require in a mentor's job description?

If you had to choose one quality as the most important for a mentor, what would it be? Why?

PAUL'S HISTORY: THE BACKGROUND OF A MENTOR?

Paul was a first-century mentor who, seeking to raise up another generation of Christian leaders, invested his life in younger men. We can learn valuable mentoring principles from his story.

First a little background. Paul was given a Hebrew name, Saul, at his birth. He was born to a Jewish family in the city of Tarsus, a port city of Turkey. It's likely that he came from a family of tentmakers, the profession he chose for himself prior to his conversion to Christianity. Paul and his family were Roman citizens (thus he also carried the Roman name Paul), but he grew up in Jerusalem. He was trained in the Jewish religion by a leading Jewish scholar named Gamaliel, and Paul later became a Pharisee, a leader among Jews. He was zealous in his Judaism—so zealous that he thought himself to be blameless according to the law. Some scholars believe Paul was a Jewish missionary who worked hard to convert Gentiles to Judaism.

Paul is perhaps better known for persecuting the young Christian church that taught Jesus was the long-awaited Messiah. With the authority and consent of the chief priest, Paul arrested believers, had them imprisoned, and consented to their deaths. He was

 You can read specific details about Paul's story in chapters 13–28 of the Book of Acts and in his letters in the New Testament.

present when Stephen was martyred, approving of his death (see Acts 7:57–8:1). Here's the way he described his own past: "I intensely persecuted God's church and tried to destroy it" (Galatians 1:13). He mistreated men and women (see Acts 22:4), punishing them in synagogues and pursuing them even to foreign cities (see Acts 26:11).

It was on the road to one of those foreign cities where Paul had a dramatic spiritual encounter. The resurrected Jesus appeared, blinded Paul with a brilliant radiance, and told him to go into the city to receive further instruction. That instruction came from a man named Ananias (see Acts 22:1-16).

Ananias was understandably hesitant to speak to Paul, given Paul's destructive history. However, God had already called Paul to be an instrument for carrying God's name to "Gentiles, kings, and the Israelites" (Acts 9:15). It was within the context of that calling that Paul poured his life into the next generation of Christian leaders.

A zealot. A persecutor. A murderer. Did you include any of those characteristics on your job description for a mentor? Surely not. Knowing Paul's biography, I almost laugh when I read one writer's words about mentors: "Keep in mind, mentors are not … perfect people."[1] Not even the best mentors come close to perfect. Mentors are often just one step ahead of their disciples. In Paul's case he had many leadership qualities, but his background was far from what you would expect for a Christian mentor.

That's great news for all of us. If perfection and a spiritual pedigree were requirements for mentors, none of us would have or be one. Many mentors are effective precisely because they've navigated tough situations in their lives. Because they've overcome their own regrettable decisions, they can lead others to do the same. Some of the best mentors I know have a deep appreciation for God's forgiving grace because they've experienced it so deeply. They've conquered their pasts through the power of God.

As you review Paul's credentials for mentoring or lack thereof, how would you say his past failings might have prepared him for the work ahead of him?

The fact that our mentors are human like us means we must be willing to grant them grace not only for the past but also in the present and the future. If we choose to work with mentors, we let go of our right to judge them for pasts that God already forgave. Today we must accept that our mentors will sin, and we'll probably see it happen. All mentors will let us down at some point. That doesn't mean they have nothing to offer us.

 A Pharisee was a member of a sect of Jewish religious leaders who emphasized the strict observance of Jewish laws and ceremonies. They often had the reputation of considering themselves more righteous than other Jews.

Accepting that our mentors will reveal their human foibles at some point is an important part of setting reasonable expectations for the relationship. Hang out with somebody long enough, and you'll see each other's weaknesses. The danger is that we may not know how to respond when the other person proves to be imperfect.

Michael Card, a Christian musician and author, wrote about his mentoring relationship with his professor, Bill Lane, in the book *The Walk*. Dr. Lane and Card met on the campus of Western Kentucky University in Bowling Green, Kentucky. Lane regularly walked the campus talking with male students he was mentoring, and he and Card walked and talked together throughout most of Card's college years. This led to a twenty-five-year relationship so deep that Michael named his oldest son after Lane. Listen to some wisdom that Card learned from his mentor:

> A true soul-friend is willing to endure the inevitable pain that is caused by being in a relationship with another human being. "We are fragile and fallen people," Bill would say. "Often we hurt each other." In a genuine relationship, friends always love and always forgive. A true soul-friend understands this and learns to rely totally on God's grace to make it possible.[2]

It's easier to forgive others when you understand and have accepted God's forgiveness as Paul did. He saw himself as the worst of sinners (see 1 Timothy 1:15-16), but he was a forgiven sinner.

When someone you're close to disappoints you, how do you forgive that person and move forward?

PAUL'S LIFE: GIVING HIMSELF

Paul invested in several first-century church leaders, including Timothy and Titus. In his mentoring relationship with Timothy, we can compare Paul's approach to mentoring with Jesus' approach.

Paul initiated the mentoring relationship.

We don't know much about the divine intersection that led to Paul's mentoring relationship with Timothy. Paul was traveling through the city of Lystra on his second missionary journey when he announced that he wanted Timothy to travel with him

Michael Card has recorded more than twenty albums and has written more than twenty books. Go to michaelcard.com to learn more. Check out his song about mentoring, "Bearers of the Light."

(see Acts 16:1-5). It's possible that Timothy converted to Christianity during Paul's first trip through Lystra on his first missionary journey, but we're not told when Timothy became a believer. We know that his mother and grandmother were believers who trained young Timothy in the Word of God (see Acts 16:1; 2 Timothy 1:3-5; 3:14-17). Timothy's father, a Greek, was likely a nonbeliever.

Timothy and Paul's mentoring relationship provides a model for us. First, Paul was one participant in Timothy's discipleship. Timothy first learned from his family, who grounded him in the Word of God. Paul built on the foundation that others gave Timothy.

Second, Paul, as the mentor, took the lead in establishing the relationship, just as Jesus took the initiative in calling His disciples. Paul apparently kept his eyes open for believers who showed promise, and Timothy caught his attention. Maybe Paul had heard from church leaders who recognized Timothy's gifts (see 1 Timothy 1:18, 4:14). No matter how Paul enlisted Timothy, he eventually came to speak of Timothy as a fellow worker in the gospel.

Taking the initiative in mentoring isn't always easy. Jesus was the Son of God. Paul was an apostle extraordinaire. Compared to them, we might struggle with whether we would be welcomed as potential mentors. How do we take the initiative in recruiting people to mentor?

The answer is simple: do it humbly. In offering ourselves and our time as mentors, we aren't saying, "I'm a growing Christian, and you're not, so I would like to show you the way." Nor are we saying, "I have a lot to offer you if you'll let me be your mentor." Instead, we say something as simple and honest as the words below:

> I believe God calls us to learn from and teach others. I don't claim to be perfect, and I have a long way to go in my Christian walk. With that in mind, I'm looking for someone to walk and work with so that we can both grow in our faith. I'm wondering if you would be willing to pray about starting a mentoring or discipling relationship with me. If so, I would be honored to help disciple you as I also try to grow in Christ.

We also see from Paul's role as Timothy's mentor that such a relationship often leads to a deeply committed connection. Scripture's general silence about Timothy's father suggests that he didn't have a strong presence in Timothy's life. The terms Paul used for Timothy show that their relationship developed into a deeply rooted father-son bond:

 When Paul wrote 1–2 Timothy, which were letters from him to his mentee, Timothy was likely serving as the pastor of the church in Ephesus.

He [Timothy] is my dearly loved and faithful child in the Lord (1 Corinthians 4:17).

Timothy, my true son in the faith (1 Timothy 1:2).

Timothy, my dearly loved son (2 Timothy 1:2).

I [Paul] constantly remember you in my prayers night and day. Remembering your tears, I long to see you so that I may be filled with joy (2 Timothy 1:3-4).

He [Timothy] has served with me in the gospel ministry like a son with a father (Philippians 2:22).

Paul went so far as to say that no one was as like-minded with him as Timothy was (see Philippians 2:19-20). Both men cared for God's people, valued the things of God more than anything, and gave evidence of their faith through holy character. Both were driven by their desires to obey the Great Commission. They worked together so that others would hear the gospel and grow in Christ. Theirs was an undeniable divine intersection.

Almost two decades ago a reserved, quiet student sat near the corner of the classroom. He never raised any questions, nor did he respond to any of my comments. I sensed that I needed to invite him to breakfast. We met, talked, prayed, and began a mentoring relationship that continues to this day. In those years we've debated, rejoiced, traveled, argued, confronted, forgiven, prayed, studied, done carpentry, played, and shared life. Our wives have become good friends. Now I claim my mentee as a son, and his children know me as Papaw Chuck. I would have missed a lot if I had ignored the burden God gave me to seek someone to mentor (including learning how to raft a river!).

What contemporary family or relational needs, similar to Timothy's possible lack of a fatherly influence, might make a mentor important in someone's life?

How would you describe the best way to invite someone to be your mentee?

Paul recognized Timothy's areas of needed growth.

If mentoring is a God-given relationship in which one growing Christian encourages and equips another believer to reach his or her potential as a disciple of Christ, the mentor needs to recognize ways the other person needs to grow. Sometimes this recognition comes through formal meetings and direct questioning, but more often it's discovered in the course of living life together.

When you read Paul's writings, you find hints about Timothy's struggles, as if you've read someone else's email reply without seeing the whole thread. Even if you don't know the details of the situation, you could make an educated guess as to what kinds of issues may have prompted the email. In the same way, Paul's writings to Timothy reveal information about Timothy.

For example, what do you surmise from these words from Paul: "Don't let anyone despise your youth" (1 Timothy 4:12)? Timothy may have been in his late twenties to midthirties when Paul wrote these words, but some believers in the church weren't ready to listen to a man this young. Timothy's perceived youth seemed to be a problem. Knowing Timothy would need to work hard to overcome this obstacle, Paul encouraged him to be an example through his speech, conduct, love, faith, and purity.

In addition, Timothy apparently battled "youthful passions" (2 Timothy 2:22). The word translated *passions* here refers to sinful desires, though it's not limited to sexual yearnings. These desires might have included useless arguing and impatience. Again, Paul reminded Timothy that he could counter his youthful desires by intentionally being gentle and patient while pursuing righteousness, faith, love, and peace—traits Paul would model in front of him.

Other writings of Paul suggest that Timothy was a timid person. Paul reminded him that "God has not given us a spirit of fear" (2 Timothy 1:7), and he warned the Corinthians not to create fear in Timothy when he visited their congregation (see 1 Corinthians 16:10).

Frequent illnesses and stomach problems also plagued Timothy (see 1 Timothy 5:23). Poor sanitation and contaminated water probably contributed to this issue. Whatever the illnesses were, they were recurrent enough that Paul was aware of them. We can't know for certain, but chronic illness may have tempted Timothy to grow discouraged and frustrated. If so, Paul could have encouraged Timothy with the lessons he had learned from his own ever-present "thorn in the flesh" (2 Corinthians 12:7).

Young. Lustful. Timid. Often ill. That's the picture of Timothy we find in Paul's writings. Yet Paul not only addressed each issue but also pushed Timothy to press on in spite of these obstacles. In the power of the Spirit and with the support of his fellow believers, Timothy could grow as a Christian leader. His mentor, Paul, would be beside him.

Where do you need to grow? Have you let your age convince you that God isn't ready to use you yet? Do you wrestle with lust? Does fear keep you from following God completely? Have recurrent struggles caused you to question God's care? Are other unnamed issues hindering your walk with God? Pray for God to send you a mentor who will recognize your need to grow and will love you anyway.

How could a mentor have helped Timothy temper the traits that might have worked against him as a leader—his youth, his passions, and his timidity?

Think about a time when someone pointed out a less-than-favorable trait in you—but in a helpful way. What made that strategy work for your benefit and growth?

Paul invited Timothy into his life.

From Paul's letters we can learn not only about Timothy's need to grow but also about Paul's role as a mentor. It's clear from Paul's writings that he opened his life to Timothy. His second letter to Timothy is considered to be Paul's last will and testament—his final words to Timothy as Paul awaited his death in a Roman prison. This letter is emotional, gripping, and personal. Read the following verses and consider the degree to which Paul shared his life with Timothy.

> You have followed my teaching, conduct, purpose, faith, patience, love, and endurance, along with the persecutions and sufferings that came to me in Antioch, Iconium, and Lystra. What persecutions I endured—and yet the Lord rescued me from them all (2 Timothy 3:10-11).

These verses read like a journal, and they're packed with details. Using nine different nouns, Paul summarized all Timothy had seen. The first seven elements are positive, showing that Timothy heard Paul's teaching, saw his obedience, witnessed his faith and persistence, and experienced his love. Young Timothy saw Christ modeled in his mentor in each of these areas:

1. *Teaching.* The gospel, Paul's message of Christ
2. *Conduct.* Paul's way of life, actions based on his beliefs
3. *Purpose.* Paul's single-minded commitment to follow Christ and make Him known
4. *Faith.* Paul's confidence in God, which was evident in his actions
5. *Patience.* Paul's long-suffering and persistence, even when others weren't cooperative
6. *Love.* Paul's *agape* love, demonstrated in the ways he loved his friends and enemies through his actions even when feelings of love weren't present
7. *Endurance.* Paul's faithfulness amid trying circumstances

Don't miss the last two nouns in Paul's list of experiences that Timothy was aware of: persecutions and sufferings (see Acts 13–14). Paul had been driven out of Pisidia, mistreated in Iconium, and stoned in Lystra. Timothy may have been present when Paul was persecuted and left for dead in Lystra. If so, he saw Paul pay a price for his faith, and yet God preserved Paul to preach again.

Timothy also knew of times when Paul was whipped, beaten with rods, and confronted with danger on all sides but still found God's strength ever present in his weakness (see 2 Corinthians 11:23-30; 12:10). Timothy, who was timid, would likely have needed to remember that testimony when he himself would be imprisoned for his faith (see Hebrews 13:23). Paul invited Timothy to the thrill of the mountaintops, and he allowed Timothy to help bear his anguish in the valleys. That's sharing life along the way.

What does it look like to invite somebody into your life? That answer varies for every mentor, but it always includes time and vulnerability. For Robert Coleman, it means regularly meeting with men and occasionally traveling with them. My wife, Pam, invites young women into our home to share lunch and conversation. David, a pastor, makes sure he doesn't carry out ministry alone; he takes someone with him wherever he goes. Kristen challenges young women to join her in her church's women's ministry. Some of my colleagues where I teach have opened their homes and invited students to live with them, get to know them, and become part of their families.

Chris James, a collegiate minister and pastor in the Northeast, is both a mentee and a mentor to me. Our paths crossed a few years ago in New Mexico, and God created a divine intersection for us. I'm privileged to walk beside Chris and encourage him in his work, and I learn from him at the same time. He's fully committed to mentoring, and his ministry now touches the world through men to whom he's given his time and energy. It was Chris who taught me that you can mentor someone in the car as you run an errand. It's amazing how much you can learn and teach in just a few minutes when you invite someone to ride with you along the way.

 Agape love denotes the special unconditional love of God. This type of love has God as its object, true motivator, and source. [3]

 The word translated *have followed* in verse 10 doesn't refer to a casual observation. It means "to follow closely, to investigate, to observe carefully."

Do you have someone who lets you get close enough to see the mountains and the valleys in his or her life?

Does the role of a mentor change when a mentee goes through an incredibly difficult experience? If so , how?

What answer would you give if someone asked why God didn't rescue him or her from life's difficulties?

Paul challenged Timothy to fulfill his calling.

These events happened almost ten years ago as I write this material, but sportscasters still occasionally remind us of these defeats. The 2008 Summer Olympics 4 x 100 relay races were disasters for the U.S. men's and women's teams. The problem wasn't that the teams weren't fast. The problem was that both teams fumbled baton transfers and never advanced beyond the semifinals. The women dropped the baton, and the men never transferred the baton cleanly. One sprinter later said, "By the time I went to grab it, there was nothing."[4] That's heartbreaking, because no matter how fast you can run, you can't win a relay race if you don't pass the baton within the passing zone.

I fear too many people might say the same thing about the church's efforts to pass the baton of leadership from one generation to the next. I have a lot of confidence and hope in the next generation of church leaders. They want to take the gospel to North American and the nations. They have a heightened awareness of the importance of practicing social ministry and social justice along with evangelism. In some ways, the reckless, trusting faith of this generation of adults puts my generation to shame.

My concern is that older church leaders aren't doing enough to pass the faith to the next generation. I sometimes wonder if young-adult Christians feel as if they're reaching back and nothing is there. Intergenerational mentoring can correct that problem.

The apostle Paul got it right. He called Timothy to travel with him and learn from him, but he made Timothy do more than observe. Paul knew Timothy was gifted, so much so that the church affirmed him and set him apart for ministry (see 1 Timothy 4:14). The apostle trained Timothy, sent him out to do ministry, and often reconnected with him between tasks.

A quick review of Timothy's work shows how much Paul trusted him. Timothy accompanied Paul on portions of two of his missionary journeys, and he accepted Paul's assignments on the apostle's behalf. Timothy and Silas stayed in Berea to minister after the crowds forced Paul to leave (see Acts 17:10-15). Later, after the men rejoined Paul in Athens, Paul sent Timothy out again to check on the churches planted in Macedonia (see 1 Thessalonians 3:1-2). When Paul couldn't go to Corinth, he sent Timothy, his "dearly loved and faithful child in the Lord" (1 Corinthians 4:17).

From prison Paul sent Timothy to Philippi to get a report on that good church (see Philippians 2:19-20). Paul also trusted Timothy to confront false teachers in the church at Ephesus (see 1 Timothy 1:3-4). Paul and Timothy were so close that six letters of the New Testament bear their names as coauthors. As we'll see, Paul very much wanted Timothy with him as he faced his impending death.

Timothy had quite a journey for the almost two decades that he served with Paul— from disciple and traveling partner to coauthor and pastor. Paul helped Timothy grow through ministry opportunities and challenges. In our world, that could mean serving as a reference, being aware of opportunities to serve, helping people network, praying for direction, and being available for counsel as needed. Mentors pave the way for their mentees to do what God has called and gifted them to do.

You may not be called to ministry in the same way Timothy was, but a mentor can play the same connecting, encouraging role in your life. Many employers provide occasional mentors or sponsor mentors to help new employees navigate internal systems and improve productivity. Some school systems require rookie teachers to work with mentor teachers who can share their experience and wisdom. Other companies use mentors to challenge long-term employees to move beyond plateau and mediocrity.

These mentors are different from what we've described so far in this study, but they can still have a significant influence. Thank God when He gives you these kinds of mentors, especially if they're believers. Occasional mentors don't typically influence our lives as Paul guided Timothy's, but God can still use them to call us to bigger things.

 The New Testament letters written by Paul and Timothy are 1–2 Thessalonians, 2 Corinthians, Philippians, Philemon, and Colossians

In your experience how effective have churches been in passing the spiritual baton to the next generation?

Why could Christian leaders struggle to pass the baton of spiritual leadership? List a few reasons.

PAUL'S DEATH: MODELING FAITH

Remember that "wow" moment I had when the conference speaker spoke about his mentor's gift of a kidney? I had another wow moment when reading Michael Card's *The Walk*. Years after Michael had graduated from college and had begun his powerful ministry career, he received a phone call from Dr. Lane. Dr. Lane, then living in Seattle while Michael lived in Franklin, Tennessee, had been diagnosed with cancer. Card describes the call this way:

> A few months later, Brenda [Dr. Lane's wife] called and proposed the idea of their moving to Franklin. During the conversation Bill told me why he wanted to spend his last days here. He didn't feel Seattle was home, even after eight years there. Neither did he want to go back to Bowling Green, even though his years there had been some of the happiest of his life. "I want to come to Franklin," he said. "I want to show you how a Christian man dies." When I hung up the phone from that conversation, I realized through deep sorrow that I had just been given the greatest compliment of my life. There was still more Bill wanted to teach, and for reasons known only to him, he wanted to teach them to me.[5]

When I read these words, I put down my book and just sat for a while with the power of what I had read. After some thought I realized that the apostle Paul did the same thing for Timothy. As Paul faced his own death, he gave Timothy his final charge in 2 Timothy 4:1-8. That charge is both a challenge to Timothy and a testimony of Paul's life. Imagine Timothy's emotions as he read these words from his mentor:

> **I solemnly charge you before God and Christ Jesus, who is going to judge the living and the dead, and because of his appearing and his kingdom: Preach the word; be ready in season and out of season; rebuke,**

For a glimpse into mentoring relationships in action, watch video session 3, "Dave, Teddy, and Patrick's Story," available at lifeway.com/mentor.

correct, and encourage with great patience and teaching. For the time will come when people will not tolerate sound doctrine, but according to their own desires, will multiply teachers for themselves because they have an itch to hear what they want to hear. They will turn away from hearing the truth and will turn aside to myths. But as for you, exercise self-control in everything, endure hardship, do the work of an evangelist, fulfill your ministry. For I am already being poured out as a drink offering, and the time for my departure is close. I have fought the good fight, I have finished the race, I have kept the faith. There is reserved for me the crown of righteousness, which the Lord, the righteous Judge, will give me on that day, and not only to me, but to all those who have loved his appearing (2 Timothy 4:1-8).

The connections between Paul's charge to Timothy and his own personal testimony are clear. Paul knew he would face the Judge of eternity, but he was prepared to do so because he had fought his fight and finished his race. He also wanted Timothy to be faithful until the end. As a prisoner being sacrificed like an offering poured out to God, Paul could call Timothy with integrity to that same level of obedience.

The apostle was ready to die, and he wouldn't miss his opportunity to teach Timothy about living and dying. Centuries later we can learn the same truths.

1. *Daily obedience prepares us for death.* Paul could truthfully say, "I have fought the good fight" (v. 7). He knew the power of wearing the full armor of God (see Ephesians 6:11). He had preached the Word, even though doing so cost him his physical freedom. Without arrogance Paul could call others to imitate him as he imitated Christ (see 1 Corinthians 11:1). Live like me, Paul said, and you'll have run the race well.

2. *We can teach others until the day we die.* Brother Jack, my pastoral mentor, shared the gospel with others until he died. Ronnie, a deacon who invested in me years ago as his young pastor, taught me about trusting God as I talked with him on the phone not long before cancer took his life. Jeannie, a model for my wife, continued to be an example of faith for her family and friends as she faced death. As long as God gives us breath, we can still teach; in fact, others might learn the most about our faith through our God-given confidence in death.

3. *Death is easier when we leave behind someone else who's ready to carry on the work of the gospel.* All of Paul's work with Timothy was tested after Paul's death. The mentor would no longer be available. Timothy would have to rely on the lessons learned; the example Paul set; and most important, the God to whom his mentor had always directed him. Paul had confidence, though, that God would complete his work through Timothy.

Paul's death was imminent, but he was at peace. His heart was clear. He had been faithful. The fight was almost over, the race almost run. He longed to see Timothy (see 2 Timothy 4:9-10), but he could rest knowing Timothy was fully prepared and willing to take over the work. Paul's son in the faith would do what he had challenged him to do:

> **You, therefore, my son, be strong in the grace that is in Christ Jesus. What you have heard from me in the presence of many witnesses, commit to faithful men who will be able to teach others also (2 Timothy 2:1-2).**

Paul's ministry would thus touch generations to come. The witness of the gospel would go on. That's a meaningful way to live and a meaningful way to die.

Paul and Timothy are examples of the wisdom of God's divine intersections. Think about it. Paul had been a murderer. Timothy was timid and sickly. By today's standards neither one would be considered an award-winning candidate to take the gospel to the nations. But God knew Paul would be an extraordinary mentor and Timothy would be a humble, teachable mentee who would then preach the Word also. Only God makes those kinds of connections.

THROUGH THE WEEK

> CONNECT: Initiate a conversation with a potential mentee.

> PRAY: Ask God to reveal your areas of needed growth.

> OBSERVE: Think about changes you need to make in your life to ensure that it will someday end well.

> READ: If you want to read about women mentoring, consider these resources:

- *Finding a Mentor, Being a Mentor* by Donna Otto
- *Transforming Together* by Ele Parrot
- *Women Leading Women* by Jaye Martin and Terri Stovall
- *Adorned: Living Out the Beauty of the Gospel Together* by Nancy DeMoss Wolgemuth
- *The Greatest Mentors in the Bible* by Tim Elmore

> A SUGGESTION FOR MENTORS: Because all of us have sinful backgrounds, continually remind your mentees what God does with our sin (see Psalm 51:9; 103:2, Isaiah 1:18; Jeremiah 31:34, Micah 7:19). Talk about ways these truths inspire and encourage you.

> A SUGGESTION FOR MENTEES: Keep handy the Bible verses about the way God forgives us. Always be ready to tell a nonbeliever about forgiveness and grace. Ask your mentor to pray for you as you seek to have that conversation with others.

1. Tim Elmore, *Lifegiving Mentors* (Duluth, GA: Growing Leaders Inc., 2008), Kindle edition, location 797.
2. Michael Card, *The Walk* (Nashville: Thomas Nelson, 2000), 46–47.
3. Chad Brand, Charles Draper, and Archie England, eds., "Love," *Holman Illustrated Bible Dictionary* (Nashville: Holman Reference, 2003), 1054.
4. Dick Patrick, "Baton Drops Mar U.S. Efforts in Both 4 x 100 Relays," August 22, 2008, http://usatoday30.usatoday.com/sports/olympics/beijing/track/2008-08-21-sprintrelays_N.htm.
5. Card, *The Walk*, 90–91.

SESSION FOUR

TAKING THE FIRST STEPS

He confronted and challenged me at the same time, and his words changed my life. I was having dinner with Robert Coleman, an author and a long-term mentor of many men over several decades. I was a young professor at the time, and Dr. Coleman had spoken in my class earlier that day. His mentee traveling with him sat at the table listening quietly as Dr. Coleman challenged me.

"You need to do the same thing I'm doing, Chuck," he told me. "You need to invest in a group of young men. Do it not because I've told you to do it but because that's the way Jesus made disciples." I wasn't sure where to begin, but I knew this man of God had challenged me to be Christlike. I couldn't ignore his words and still be a man of integrity. I knew I had to begin somewhere.

The goal of this session's study is to help you know how to begin, first as a mentee. The following steps outline the way to start as someone who's being mentored and grow toward being a mentor. The steps might not always occur in this order, but they outline a start toward healthy mentoring relationships.

STEP 1: BE OPEN; ONE SIZE DOESN'T FIT ALL

Writing about mentoring can be complex because there are many kinds of mentors. One book, in fact, lists three types of mentors and eight different mentoring functions within those types.[1] *Intensive mentors*—the kind of mentor we most often talk about in this study—deliberately and intentionally invest in another life with regularity. Mutual commitment, direction, motivation, and growth are primary goals of the relationship. Jesus and Paul are examples of this kind of mentor.

Occasional mentors are available to help for short periods of time in particular ways, and they complement rather than replace intensive mentors. I have a long-term friend to whom I turn whenever I have financial questions. He's not a CPA or a professional financial adviser, but he has a business background. He knows me well, so he understands my comfort level with taking financial risks. I also trust him with our financial information. We don't usually talk about other issues to this level, but he's always the person I consult for financial guidance. That's an occasional mentor.

Passive mentors are role models who give us guidance, even though they often do so from a distance, and they probably don't know they're our mentors. These mentors might be sports heroes, politicians, or pastors. Some passive mentors are already gone, and we learn from them through their writings or biographies. Charles Spurgeon and David Platt are two men I consider my passive mentors. Women like missionaries Lottie Moon and Amy Carmichael, in addition to speakers and writers like Beth Moore and Priscilla Shirer, are passive mentors for women I know.

Why is it important to recognize different types of mentors? Because you may not always have an intensive mentor. You might look for someone to invest deeply in your life but be unable to find that person right away. Instead, someone who loves to pray might want to show you how to talk to God. Somebody else may be available for occasional vocational counseling but not for long-term Christian discipleship. If you can't find all you want in a mentoring relationship, don't get discouraged. Thank God for the gifts of people He places in your path and continue to watch patiently for an intensive mentor. It never hurts to walk briefly in the shadows of several people along the way.

We also may need different types of mentors because no one mentor can give us all the support we need to live an effective Christian life. Every mentor has strengths

 Learn about the global impact of Charles Spurgeon's and David Platt's ministries at spurgeon.org and radical.net, respectively.

and weaknesses—weaknesses we can overcome by finding other mentors to help us in those areas. My mentor, Brother Jack, was a great mentor as I wrestled with God's calling on my life. When I had questions about education, though, he wasn't the best person to help because he had completed graduate school several decades before I was born. With wisdom and humility he encouraged me to find a more recent graduate to help me with those questions as an occasional mentor.

When you consider the kind of spiritual guidance you need, what would be the benefits of having several occasional mentors?

Think about the passive mentors in your life. What specific areas of spiritual growth have they helped you develop?

STEP 2: START WITH YOUR FAITH COMMUNITY

You can find a mentor in many places, but the local church is the place to start. The Bible uses dozens of images to describe the church, but one of the most prominent images is the body of Christ (see Romans 12:4-8; 1 Corinthians 12:12-26; Ephesians 4:15-16). This image is a powerful picture of a church marked by unity in diversity.

If you think about it, the church is incredible. Its members come from diverse backgrounds and varied cultures. We're economically, educationally, and vocationally different. Sometimes we're racially and ethnically distinct from one another. Many were raised in church, but others are new to the church world. Seldom do we all read from the same version of the Bible or agree on every theological detail. Nevertheless, God somehow takes all this diversity, unites the believers around Christ, and makes us one body.

We're one, and yet we're different. You might be an ear or an eye in the body, but all of us are in the body according to God's plan (see 1 Corinthians 12:11,18). Think about the diversity in your own church—different gifts, different strengths, different callings, different backgrounds. The Holy Spirit puts the church together as He wills, and His plan is always right (see 1 Corinthians 12:4-12). Within that plan are all kinds of potential mentors.

I'm particularly intrigued by Paul's words about church members who feel less significant:

Those parts of the body that are weaker are indispensable. And those parts of the body that we consider less honorable, we clothe these with greater honor, and our unrespectable parts are treated with greater respect, which our respectable parts do not need. Instead, God has put the body together, giving greater honor to the less honorable, so that there would be no division in the body, but that the members would have the same concern for each other (1 Corinthians 12:22-25).

It's important to catch what Paul said here: God gives even more attention to the weak and insignificant so that they understand their value in the church. Just as we devote extra time and energy to fix the blotches and blemishes on our bodies, God devotes Himself to those who see themselves as weak or minor parts of the church.

Years ago I was training believers in a part of the world where being a Christian is risky. Many of them were physically weak, having little to eat because of poverty. Some, both male and female, bore the scars of physical persecution. They struggled to communicate with me in broken English. I learned during the week, though, that these men and women knew more about faith than I did. Were they weak? Yes. Did they find their strength in God? Absolutely. Did they teach me in their circumstances? Without question.

God blends the church together so that the strong help the weak, the older teach the younger, the more presentable give attention to the less presentable, and all rejoice and weep together. To put it another way, God created the church in such a way that He expects us to invest in one another. Mentoring through the local church matters, so begin there when you look for a mentor.

Where do you think you fit in as a part of the body of Christ?

Read 1 Corinthians 12:7-21. What gifts do you have to offer the church?

 Interested in learning more about images of the church in the New Testament? Check out Mark Dever's chapter in *A Theology for the Church* (ed. Daniel Akin, B&H Academic, 2014).

STEP 3: TRUST GOD FOR GUIDANCE

We've already learned in this study that both Jesus and Paul initiated relationships with their mentees. That's not to say, however, that mentees should never seek a mentor. God can use the one being mentored to challenge a potential mentor to give his life to another person.

That's the way it worked for Michael Card. Michael wanted to spend time with Bill Lane, and he first asked Dr. Lane's wife whether Bill might be available. Mrs. Lane encouraged Michael to ask Bill. Mrs. Lane knew Bill had been waiting for someone to approach him. He always believed that God would prompt the right young man to ask for his time and that the Lord's timing was best. When Michael asked, Dr. Lane was ready.[2]

That's also the way it worked in my life with young men like Nicholas and Brian. Both came to me seeking a mentor, and each took the risk to ask. Both gave me an out from the beginning ("I understand if you don't have time"), but the passion of their interest caught my attention. To be honest, I didn't have much margin for more mentees at the time, but God convinced me through His Word and His Spirit to give time to these men.

My relationship with Chris, a missionary now serving in a high-security part of the world, began at his initiative and has become an example of a how a mentoring relationship changes. As a student, he and I regularly met over the course of several years in an intensive mentoring connection. Geographical miles eventually changed that, and now I'm an occasional mentor for him. Even though we don't meet regularly, I pray for him regularly. We use Skype or email whenever Chris wants to hang out via cyberspace. The blessing of the Internet makes it possible for a mentor to engage in along-the-way discipleship in a unique way.

Trusting God to direct you to a mentor doesn't mean you're not involved in the process. Even as you look to God for guidance, use the following practical steps to help you get started.

Create a wish list.

If you think about all the characteristics you might want in a mentor, you would be alert for someone who is—

• mature but growing;
• truthful but fun;
• persistent but patient;
• prayerful but confident;

- detailed but goal-oriented;
- forgiving but demanding;
- listening but advising;
- encouraging but challenging;
- empathetic but teaching;
- spiritually strong but dependent on God;
- knowledgeable but learning;
- available but stewarding time wisely.

If you look for somebody who meets all of these qualifications, of course, you'll never find a mentor. So what should you look for in a mentor? Here are my starting points.

1. *My mentor must be the same gender.* Another man will better understand the issues I face and help protect me from the temptations inherent in male-female relationships. The last place I want to invite trouble is in a mentoring relationship.

2. *My mentor should be growing in Christ, particularly in areas where I need to grow.* His walk with God should both challenge and encourage me.

3. *I want a mentor with whom I share some common interests.* If my mentor isn't a friend with whom I enjoy spending time, the mentoring won't last long. I would look for someone with whom I would enjoy talking and taking a walk.

4. *I want to follow someone who's known for his prayer life.* Because I'm well aware of spiritual warfare, I want my mentor to be a prayer warrior on my behalf. I want to know that he knows how to touch heaven from his knees.

5. *I would seek a mentor who's respected by others yet exhibits Christian humility.* If he has his own mentors to whom he's accountable, that would be even better. I want to walk along the way with a mentor who's still learning from others.

6. *My mentor should be a positive person.* He must not be easily discouraged. He must be someone who sees reality for what it is, at the same time recognizing what God might be doing in a mentee's life. A good mentor will see in me what I can't see in myself.

7. *I want a mentor who has time for mentoring.* We may not meet every week, but I want to know that we can meet on a regular schedule. If he's too busy for regular meetings, I need him to be honest with me about his limitations.

You may not always find someone who meets every expectation, but aim high as you establish your wish list for a mentor. Look for a growing Christian whose life you want to emulate.

Start fishing in the right ponds.

Start with your local church and learn whether a staff member would be willing to mentor you. If not, don't be disappointed, because staff members are often very busy. Use the opportunity, though, to ask whether your church-staff member can suggest someone who might have time to work with you. When staff members are unavailable, look around for a committed layperson who might be a mentor.

A small group in your local church is another place to look for a mentor. Make sure you're involved in a small group that offers Bible teaching, Christian fellowship, prayer support, and ministry opportunities. That group might be a Sunday School class, a home group, a men's ministry, or a women's ministry. Get to know people in the group and stay alert for prospective mentors.

If there are Christians in your workplace, you might also find a mentor there. Learn to listen, watch, and pray while you're working. Listen for evidence of coworkers who are Christians. Observe the way they relate to people and respond to difficulties; look for evidence of a Christian spirit. Pray for God to direct you to others with whom you might have a mentoring relationship.

A sometimes overlooked but valuable option for finding a mentor is your family. Indeed, Christian mothers and fathers should first focus on mentoring their own children. If you want to surprise your parent, ask him or her to meet with you weekly to show you how to be a faithful follower of God. Even if you ask a parent for guidance in only one area of your life, that kind of mentoring has matchless value. Siblings can be great mentors as well.

I encourage you also not to ignore the Internet as a possible means of finding a mentor. One of my mentees, Merrick, first connected with me through an online class. Even today we most often connect through the web and the telephone. There are all kinds of mentors and all kinds of places to find a mentor. So take the initiative to get the process started.

What are the first three characteristics that come to mind when you consider what you want in a mentor?

As you review your life patterns, all the ponds you swim in, where are you most likely to find the kind of mentor you described in the previous question?

Plan your first contact.

I'm an introvert by nature. I enjoy teaching classes, but I don't really enjoy an event that requires me to mingle and talk. I can do it, but it's not easy for me. For the most part, I'm not someone who naturally takes the initiative to start a relationship. Consequently, making contact isn't easy for me. Some mentors want to be asked, but making that contact is more difficult for some than for others. Nevertheless, finding a mentor sometimes requires you to make the first move.

Howard Hendricks, a longtime professor at Dallas Theological Seminary, provides some practical ways to make contact with a mentor in his excellent book *As Iron Sharpens Iron.* Here are a few of his ideas that might work for you.

- *Go through the front door.* Simply contact a potential mentor and ask for an appointment.
- *Use a go-between person to set up a meeting.* Take advantage of relational networks to spend time with a prospective mentor.
- *Recognize a potential mentor for something he or she has done and ask to learn from him or her.* For example, compliment your Bible study teacher and ask for time to dig more deeply into the topic.
- *Offer to serve in a ministry or project in order to work alongside someone who could be a mentor.* Learn from him. Listen to him. Talk to him.
- *Open a conversation by asking a prospective mentor about the people who've most influenced his or her life.* He or she will likely ask you about the same issue, and you can then talk about mentoring.[3]

Here's a strategy that works for me. When I meet a man from whom I would like to learn, I invite him to breakfast or lunch (it's easier for me to carry on a conversation over a meal). In that first meeting I thank him for his Christian witness and ask whether we could meet monthly for a meal just to talk. We wouldn't have an agenda. There would be no planning or homework. Just talking. Time together—that's all I ask for.

In some cases the person is too busy to meet monthly. Most of the time, though, that first meal has led to some type of mentoring relationship. Sometimes we meet quarterly; sometimes monthly; and on occasion, weekly, but the meal has become a regular occurrence in many cases.

STEP 4: DISCUSS YOUR EXPECTATIONS

One of the most common problems in mentoring relationships, as in other ongoing relationships, is unmet expectations. Discussing expectations at the start can protect the relationship from hurt feelings and awkwardness later. Here are some expectations worth discussing.

Formal or Informal?

The following lists outline the differences between formal and informal mentoring. Most mentoring relationships have elements of both, and both are effective ways to mentor. Indeed, the best mentoring has the informality of a strong relationship, coupled with the formality of intentional goals toward spiritual growth. What matters is that both the mentor and the mentee understand the nature of the relationship.

Informal:
• Relationships are often spontaneous; chemistry is important.
• Casual, unplanned meetings occur.
• Agenda is determined by immediate need; any topic is open.
• Goals are often unstated.
• The relationships are often lifelong.
• Evaluation seldom happens.

Formal:
• Relationships are often set up by a supervisor or leader.
• Regular meetings occur.
• An agenda is set, often with intentional teaching.
• Goals are established.
• A time duration is set.
• Intentional evaluations are scheduled.

What I argue for is goal-oriented informality that combines both styles. David and I have this kind of relationship. We meet at least monthly to talk about life and ministry. He brings a list of questions he wants to discuss, and we know we typically have one hour to cover these details in a formal meeting. At the same time, our families occasionally have lunch together, and we share life together in an informal way.

I enjoy the formal meeting times with my mentees, but some of our best times occur when we travel together to churches or conferences where I'm speaking. We spend hours in a car or plane talking about God, marriage, missions, and callings. Sometimes we just hang out and bowl, play putt-putt golf, run, hike, camp, eat, and talk. I've learned that some young men are more willing to talk honestly in an informal setting than they are in my office.

 For a glimpse into a mentoring relationship in action, watch video session 4, "Carrie and Courtney's Story," available at lifeway.com/mentor.

Each mentoring relationship is different. My preference is to meet in a formal setting no less than every other week, although some situations can afford only monthly meetings. With the Internet and mobile communications available today, mentors and mentees can still easily keep in touch between scheduled meetings.

When I'm mentoring, my goal is at least two formal meetings and two informal get-togethers each month. The formal meetings are usually forty-five to sixty minutes long. The informal times might be as simple as eating lunch, running an errand, watching a ball game, or taking a walk.

This formal-informal combination has always worked well for me. The formal meetings provide an opportunity for the mentee to show his commitment to the relationship. If he always shows up prepared to talk about the issue at hand, I know he has dedicated time and energy to the relationship. At the same time, the informal times are my opportunity to show the mentee that I'm equally committed to the relationship. These casual times are sometimes time-consuming and costly, but I want my mentee to know that I enjoy just hanging out apart from our official meeting times. The informal times move us beyond professor and student and help solidify our relationship as Christian brothers and friends.

The mentor and the mentee must decide how often they'll meet, determine the schedule up front, and strive to meet those expectations. The schedule might change at times, but if the mentoring relationship has no established meeting expectations, it often fails to get started at all.

Goals

Tim Elmore, the founder and president of Growing Leaders Incorporated, has committed his life to training leaders—especially young leaders. He writes that a mentor's goal should be to help mentees do these five things:

1. *Discover strengths.* Find out what they do well and strive to make that ability even stronger.
2. *Develop character.* Grow morally.
3. *Determine focus.* Narrow their concentration to grow deeply in one area, such as education, career, or Christian walk.
4. *Discern blind spots.* Be self-aware with the help of others.
5. *Close the gap between potential and performance.* Become all they can be.[4]

This list may not be comprehensive, but it's a helpful start for thinking about the primary goals of a mentoring relationship. When I first meet with a potential mentee, I invite him to write a description of what he would want our relationship to be if he could design it. In his "The sky's the limit" proposal, I ask him to tell me how often he wants to meet, topics he might want to address, things he might want to do, any concerns he has, and anything else he wants me to know. That proposal is our starting point for determining what the mentoring relationship will look like.

I first compare my mentee's proposal with Elmore's list to make sure he has identified most things that need to be addressed. Most mentees, for example, don't include discerning blind spots as one of his or her goals (after all, that's why they're called blind spots). Others want to focus on their recognized weaknesses but don't think much about building their strengths. Using the mentee's proposal, Elmore's list, and my schedule and availability, we then work together to set a direction so that both of us share the same expectations. My goal is to do my best to meet those expectations.

Assessment Times

A lack of evaluation is one weakness of most mentoring relationships. Businesspeople in formal mentoring settings are good at evaluation, but others seldom take time to evaluate the relationship. Reviews can make for an awkward conversation, and many of us are unpracticed at having those difficult conversations when someone doesn't meet our expectations. The result is a mentoring relationship that isn't as strong as it could be.

A mentoring relationship doesn't require a long, extensive evaluation. Instead, I suggest a simple one-on-one verbal evaluation that takes place every six months. Both the mentor and the mentee should answer these basic questions:

• In what ways is or isn't this mentoring relationship meeting your expectations?
• In what ways are you a stronger believer because of this mentoring relationship?
• What would you change about the way our relationship is working?
• How can I be a better mentor or mentee?
• Do you want to continue this mentoring relationship?
• If so, what should be our focus during the next six months?

These questions not only allow you to identify ways to improve the relationship but also give each mentoring partner a way out if he or she chooses not to continue. An honest exit is always much better than dropping out without explanation.

What might cause someone to drop out of a mentoring relationship?

What do you consider to be the most important expectations to be discussed between a mentor and a mentee?

STEP 5: START LOOKING FOR A MENTEE

Mentoring is about reproduction. Multiplication. Growing influence. Making disciples. It's about finding someone like Paul in your life, someone to learn from, so that you in turn can teach a Timothy, someone who can learn from you. If you're being mentored and the process stops with you, you'll miss a major principle of mentoring: there's no end to the process of reproducing disciples.

If you're looking for someone to mentor, consider these four ideas:

1. *Seek someone who shows an interest in learning and an enthusiasm for Christian growth.* Watch for others whose commitment is evident in their attendance and participation in your group.

2. *Notice who's already hanging around you.* You might find somebody in your small group, for example, who's already looking to you for guidance even though you didn't recognize that fact.

3. *Look for a potential mentee who shares your Christian values.* Push him or her to become more Christlike in the same way your mentor is pushing you.

4. *Seek a mentee who's willing to invest in somebody else.* Keep the cycle of discipleship going by recruiting mentees who understand their responsibility to reproduce themselves.[5]

However, there's another side to this coin. It's always possible that God might want you to mentor someone whose faith is wavering and whose witness is weak. He or she may be on the verge of dropping out of Christian fellowship and in desperate need of someone to connect with. God may call you to invest in him or her because He has a plan that you don't know yet. It's important to make that choice based on God's guidance—not simply a desire to rescue someone but a desire to *invest* in his or her life.

Begin asking God to direct you to someone you might mentor. You won't know all you need to know, but remember that mentoring sometimes means you're only one step ahead of your mentee. As long as you're growing in Christ—especially if you have a Paul in your life—you'll have something to give to a younger believer.

Pamela and Danny have been great examples of this truth. I met Pamela many years ago in college. She was an older student who had returned to college—and more recently, to a renewed commitment to God—after a failed relationship and the birth of a child. She had chosen to trust God and remain faithful to Him at a time when anger could have consumed her. Although she was still learning how to follow God again, she had something to offer young women because of what she had already learned from her mistakes.

Danny reaffirmed his commitment to God after living a life of promiscuity for several years. His renewed faith was fresh, alive, and contagious, and his spiritual fire was so bright that others took note. Danny taught them as much as he could, even though he was still a spiritual baby. Only a step ahead—that's all that matters!

If you're just getting started in mentoring, think about mentoring someone in one of your particular areas of strength. Maybe you're good at evangelizing; if so, teach somebody else how to do that. If Bible study or prayer comes easily for you, find somebody who can learn from you. Wherever you're growing, turn and teach someone else.

What past mistakes or difficulties can you use as tools to mentor others?

What changes do you need to make that would prepare you to mentor someone?

STEP 6: DEVELOP A WRITTEN AGREEMENT

Bill Bright founded the Campus Crusade for Christ ministry, now known as CRU. When Bill was a young believer, he wrote and signed a contract with God. He and his wife agreed to follow Christ in "total, absolute, irrevocable surrender."[6] Your mentoring covenant might not rise to that magnitude, but your commitment to a mentoring relationship should be no less serious.

Here's a sample covenant to consider at the beginning of the mentoring relationship and to reconsider during each evaluation.

> As a mentor, I agree to model Christian living, teach God's Word, and pray for my mentees. I'll provide accountability while offering guidance in living a holy life. I promise to prioritize our scheduled meetings, and I'll seek ways to share life with my mentees. My commitment is to train those I mentor and release them to train others for God's glory.

> As a mentee, I commit to attend our meetings, have a teachable spirit, strive for growth in my Christian walk, and be honest in all discussions with my mentor. I'll complete all studies as assigned and submit to accountability from my mentor. I commit to pray for my mentor and for potential mentees I might lead. My commitment is to learn and then to train others for God's glory.

STEP 7: ESTABLISH A PRAYER TRIAD

It's so basic that you might forget: prayer is essential to the mentoring process. God divinely intersects your life with the lives of your mentor and mentee. He uses each of you to urge the others toward Christlikeness. Meanwhile, the enemy stands ready to oppose. We must pray for one another. Pray for yourself. Pray for your Paul. Pray for your Timothy. Pray for the person who will be the next Timothy for your Timothy. Get together with two other people and intercede for one another as you obey Christ's command to make disciples.

THROUGH THE WEEK

> **PRAY:** If you already know someone who's in a mentoring relationship, pray for him or her daily.

> **SERVE:** Talk to a church-staff member to learn about opportunities for you to better serve your congregation.

> **CONNECT:** Reach out to a seemingly insignificant person in your faith community.

> **A SUGGESTION FOR MENTORS:** Take time to read Robert Coleman's book *The Master Plan of Evangelism*. It will challenge and inspire you.

> **A SUGGESTION FOR MENTEES:** Write your own mentoring covenant. Use it as a template for future mentoring relationships.

1. Robert Clinton, *Connecting* (Colorado Springs: NavPress, 1992).
2. Michael Card, *The Walk* (Nashville: Thomas Nelson, 2000), Kindle edition, location 137–39.
3. Howard and William Hendricks, *As Iron Sharpens Iron* (Chicago: Moody, 1995), 88-94.
4. Tim Elmore, *Lifegiving Mentors* (Duluth, GA: Growing Leaders Inc., 2008), Kindle edition, location 1249–83.
5. Ibid., location 870.
6. Bill and Vonette Bright, "Our Contract with God," March 2, 2002, https://www.generouschurch.com/357.

SESSION FIVE

DEVELOPING A
PLAN OF ACTION

I've seen it happen several times. I teach a conference about mentoring, and church members make a commitment to invest in the lives of others. Everything starts well. The first meetings are exciting, and believers begin to experience victory and renewed joy. Church leaders begin to advertise the mentoring program as a success. Members line up for mentors. Then I learn a few months later that what started so well didn't last very long.

All mentoring relationships can fall prey to this problem. We may have a good start, but then the process founders. What seemed exciting at the beginning loses its appeal. Without a plan in place for continued growth, meetings become monotonous and draining. Sometimes the relationships simply fade.

That's not the aim, of course. The goal is to make disciples who'll teach others, who'll teach yet another generation of disciples. To get there, however, we need a strategy. This session offers some suggestions for developing lasting mentoring relationships.

PREPARE FOR SPIRITUAL BATTLE

The apostle Paul, as a mentor to Timothy, Titus, and others, understood the realities of spiritual warfare. He knew that Christians wrestle against rulers, authorities, world powers of darkness, and spiritual forces of evil (see Ephesians 6:12). This spiritual battle is real, and it's intense.

We see evidence of this spiritual conflict all around us. Churches engage in conflict over trivial things, weakening the church's united witness (see John 17:20-21). The enemy does all he can to sow seeds of discord among Christians and breed jealousy, bitterness, and internal strife. He knows a divided church has little to offer to an already fractured world. False teaching worms its way in, and God's people are sometimes arrogant and rebellious. As a result, we get distracted from doing the work of the Great Commission (see Matthew 28:18-20).

We find evidence of spiritual warfare inside us too. The enemy tries to entice us into old behaviors, luring us into patterns of our old lives before Christ (see Ephesians 4:17-32). At times, choosing our way over God's becomes so routine that we think we'll never have spiritual victory. Sometimes we wonder whether our spiritual experience is authentic at all. After influencing us to sin, the enemy then heaps guilt on us; the tempter quickly becomes the accuser (see Revelation 12:10). "God doesn't love you anymore; He will never use you now," he says. His strategy often leads to a cycle of defeat and discouragement.

In light of all this, we need to learn how to wear God's armor. In *Discipled Warriors* I tell the story of Tim, a young believer whose church didn't disciple him.[1] Other believers told him what he needed to do (read the Bible, pray, and witness), but they didn't show him how. Nobody taught him how to live victoriously in Christ. As a result, he lived a defeated Christian life, even though his church placed him in leadership and teaching positions. Tim's story may sound familiar to many of us.

For undiscipled believers, the enemy's arrows strike with doubt, discouragement, and loneliness. That's where mentors become critical. Mentors guard their mentees against the enemy's attacks while teaching their disciples to stand in God's power against Satan. Mentors deflect the enemy's arrows until their mentees have learned how to fight on their own.

The enemy can still win temporarily, of course. He knows where you're vulnerable, including areas your mentor may not be aware of. You'll likely fall in some battles. When that happens, your mentor's job is to pick you up and help you walk forward again. You never fight the war alone if you have a mentor by your side. God gives us each other to get ready for battle.

In what ways are you aware of the enemy's attacks?

Who picks you up when you fall?

WEAR GOD'S ARMOR

My father was a volunteer firefighter, and I grew up wanting to be just like him. As a preschooler, I tried my best to wear his boots around the house. It wasn't until I became a firefighter myself, though, that I understood how important that gear really was. Everything from the boots to the helmet is designed to protect firefighters as they wage war against the flames. Firefighting requires months of training to learn how to use the equipment and protective outerwear. Firefighters must trust their equipment as they enter burning buildings, and no smart firefighters would work without it.

Our spiritual battle is the same. Paul told us that we prepare for this battle by putting on the full armor of God:

> Be strengthened by the Lord and by his vast strength. Put on the full armor of God so that you can stand against the schemes of the devil. For our struggle is not against flesh and blood, but against the rulers, against the authorities, against the cosmic powers of this darkness, against evil, spiritual forces in the heavens. For this reason take up the full armor of God, so that you may be able to resist in the evil day, and having prepared everything, to take your stand. Stand, therefore, with truth like a belt around your waist, righteousness like armor on your chest, and your feet sandaled with readiness for the gospel of peace. In every situation take up the shield of faith with which you can extinguish all the flaming arrows of the evil one. Take the helmet of salvation and the sword of the Spirit—which is the word of God. Pray at all times in the Spirit with every prayer and request, and stay alert with all perseverance and intercession for all the saints (Ephesians 6:10-18).

 "Be sober-minded, be alert. Your adversary the devil is prowling around like a roaring lion, looking for anyone he can devour" (1 Peter 5:8).

God outfits us for the spiritual battle we're engaged in, but knowing how to use that gear requires training. God's plan is for more mature believers to teach younger believers how to use the equipment and protection He provides. That's New Testament discipleship. That's mentoring.

As you read the following descriptions of the armor of God, keep in mind that it's not separate pieces. It's all connected around God's Word. Also remember that training to wear and use God's armor is more than simply teaching a lesson. Effective mentoring requires sharing life. As mentors and mentees walk together, they learn to wear the armor of God every day.

The Belt of Truth

Wearing the belt of truth means knowing the Truth (Jesus), reading the truth (the Scriptures), and living the truth (a life of integrity). All three are essential. I've learned that the very essence of mentoring—walking with someone and helping that person grow spiritually—helps mentors and mentees live in the truth. Why? Being a mentor pushes us to be diligent in our own spiritual walk. As mentors, we must be on our guard against anything less than truthfulness in our words and lifestyles because we want to be examples. Mentees in turn want to honor and please their mentors. As one friend said it for me, "We live differently when we know others are watching." Being mentees and mentors makes us more conscious of whether we're living in the truth.

Mentoring relationships can get complicated because living in the truth sometimes requires questioning or confrontation. Sometimes we disagree on exactly what the truth is in a situation or what an interpretation of Scripture should be. Sometimes both mentoring partners have to ask tough questions in order to move ahead. Consider these points as you establish your mentoring relationship so that you can both live in the truth:

1. *Be clear about expectations in your commitment to the truth.* As the person being mentored, how vulnerable are you willing to be? Are you open about ways you're working out the truth of the Scriptures in your life? How deeply do you let your mentor inquire before you consider him to be prying?

2. *Remember that mentoring relationships function not only to prevent sin but also to promote growth.* Talk about proactively engaging in spiritual disciplines as much as you discuss avoiding temptations or identifying sin in each other's lives.

3. *Whatever parameters you set for the relationship, determine up front that you'll both be honest.* Any issues you hide are the very ones about which you need the most accountability. If you or your mentor finds yourself covering something up, it's time to check in with the other person.

4. *Understand that speaking the truth to each other and calling each other deeper into the truth are part of a process.* This process requires trust, and instantaneous trust is unrealistic. It develops over time and with experience. Give each other room to be human as you walk together. Ultimately, it's the Holy Spirit's role to convict us of sin, but we can encourage each other to be open to hearing the truth of the Spirit.

The Breastplate of Righteousness

Christians are righteous because God has given us His righteousness (see 2 Corinthians 5:21). Because of Christ's work on the cross, we're made righteous. At the same time, God calls us to live righteously. That is, we show God's work in our lives by making holy choices. The person who wears the breastplate of righteousness lives according to God's standards.

Scripture clearly shows us we're to help each other live righteously, and the words sound much like mentoring:

> **Encourage one another and build each other up (1 Thessalonians 5:11).**
>
> **Confess your sins to one another and pray for one another (James 5:16).**
>
> **Let us watch out for one another to provoke love and good works (Hebrews 10:24).**
>
> **Brothers and sisters, if someone is overtaken in any wrongdoing, you who are spiritual, restore such a person with a gentle spirit, watching out for yourselves so that you also won't be tempted (Galatians 6:1).**

In mentoring relationships we hold each other accountable to God's Word, push for holiness, and pick up each other when we fall. This is one area where mentors must be especially willing to be vulnerable. If mentors are unwilling to be held accountable, it's hard for them to hold others accountable. Mutual holiness must be the goal.

I have accountability partners in addition to the people I mentor, but I also give my mentees permission to ask me at any time about my Bible reading, my prayer time, my evangelism, and my personal holiness. If I know they might ask me at any point, I'm forced to strive for faithfulness all the time instead of just in the thirty minutes before our meeting. Do you have someone who holds you accountable at all times?

One exercise I've found helpful in wearing the breastplate is a sin-pattern analysis. Many of us deal with particular sin issues, and our struggles with those sins often follow a pattern. Sometimes we're more susceptible when we're physically tired. We might be more under attack when we're alone. In some cases being with the wrong people increases our vulnerability. Maybe we're more under attack at night than during the day or most defenseless when we haven't been faithfully reading the Word. When you and your mentor work together to identify these patterns in your life, you're more prepared to wear the breastplate of righteousness.

What factors make all of us fall more easily?

Where are the cracks in your armor, the areas where you need the greatest amount of accountability?

The Shoes of the Gospel of Peace

Several years ago I was traveling with Travis, one of my mentees. We stopped at a fast-food restaurant for a quick hamburger on the way to a conference where I was speaking. A man sitting at the next table unexpectedly began talking to us. "Tell me why, when you tell the truth, things don't always go right," he said.

That was a strange way to start a conversation. We learned that our new friend had just been released from prison, had been honest on all his job applications, but hadn't been hired yet. He was frustrated and hurt.

Travis jumped at the opportunity: "Would you mind if I took a few minutes and told you what gives me hope when life is tough?" He then told the story of Jesus while I drew a simple gospel illustration on a napkin. Our friend didn't choose to follow Christ then, but he heard the good news because Travis was prepared to share it.

For a glimpse into a mentoring relationship in action, watch video session 5, "Arliss and Linda's Story," available at lifeway.com/mentor.

That's what it means to wear the shoes of the gospel of peace—always being ready to share the gospel. Travis was ready, not only because he had been trained in evangelism but also because one of our mentoring goals was to be alert for opportunities to share Christ. We had been praying Colossians 4:2-4 for each other, asking God to open doors for us to practice evangelism. Both of us wanted to be faithful that day, not only to please God but also to encourage each other.

That's New Testament mentoring. Ask your mentor and/or mentees to join you in praying for opportunities, clarity, and boldness to share the gospel (see Ephesians 6:18-20; Colossians 4:2-4).

The Shield of Faith

What do you think of when you think of faith? Is it just believing? Is it trusting? Is it doing something? Paul used the illustration of a shield to help us understand faith. In Paul's day Roman soldiers covered their shields with leather and soaked them in water to defend against the enemy's flaming arrows. They were to press forward in war, not allowing the enemy's attack to hinder their forward progress.

Using that image, Paul called believers to take up the shield of faith, meaning we're to trust the truths and promises of God's Word when the enemy aims his arrows at us. Faith means we press on regardless of the opposition's ferocity, and that's much easier if we know we're not alone.

Mentors help strengthen our faith by offering the voice of God when the enemy's voice is loud. We thus learn to hear our mentor's voice in a unique, powerful way. Michael Card describes his response to the voice of his mentor this way:

> From that moment, though I barely knew him [Dr. Lane], I experienced something unique about our relationship. My ears seemed to be tuned to his voice. I am, even today, able to recall practically everything he said to me. It was as if God had designed my ears to receive this man's wisdom.[2]

An effective mentor encourages more loudly than the enemy discourages, strengthens more faithfully than the enemy weakens, and affirms more clearly than the enemy condemns. The enemy's arrows are often lies that strike at our self-understanding and ultimately work to diminish our faith. If we accept his lies as truth, the result is a defeated life. Here are some examples of ways mentors can use God's Word to bring clarity to faith when the enemy attacks.

1. The enemy's message: "God won't forgive you for what you've done."

   The Word: **"If we confess our sins, he is faithful and righteous to forgive us our sins and to cleanse us from all unrighteousness" (1 John 1:9).**

   The mentor's response: "God forgives you; let's start over again."

2. The enemy's message: "You don't mean anything to anyone."

   The Word: **"God loved the world in this way: He gave his one and only Son, so that everyone who believes in him will not perish but have eternal life" (John 3:16).**

   The mentor's response: "God loves you, and I do too."

Ask God to intersect your world with someone who can help you counter the lies of the enemy. Your victories will enable you, in turn, to help somebody else overcome the same deceptions.

The Helmet of Salvation

Ask most people what Christians mean by the term *salvation,* and I suspect they would mention eternity in heaven. Being saved is probably understood to be more about escaping hell than about living for God today. Salvation, of course, means eternity with God, but in the Bible the idea is much broader than that. Salvation in the armor-of-God passage isn't so much about our final salvation in heaven but about having victory every day through Christ. It's about conquering sin in the present tense.

Living in the here and now in our Christian lives means recognizing our identity in Christ, knowing who we are and what we've experienced in Jesus. The Bible gives us great news about who we are:

• Children of God (see John 1:12)
• Chosen by God (see John 15:16)
• At peace with God (see Romans 5:1)
• Free from condemnation (see Romans 8:1-2)
• A temple of God, a dwelling place for God's Spirit (see 1 Corinthians 3:16)
• A member of God's body (see 1 Corinthians 12:27)
• Sealed by God's Spirit (see 2 Corinthians 1:22)
• Adopted by God (see Ephesians 1:4-5)
• Citizens of heaven (see Philippians 3:20)
• Rescued, redeemed, and forgiven (see Colossians 1:13-14)
• Born of God (see 1 John 5:1)

This is unbelievable news. We're all sinners who choose to rebel against God, but God loved us so much that He sent His Son to die for us. Through Jesus we're rebels now redeemed. Sinners now made secure. Liars now loved. Idolaters now intimate with God. God loves us in spite of our history.

Although many of us can speak this language, we still don't live in victory every day. That's where mentors can make a difference. Mentors remind us every day that we each matter to someone—our mentors—because we first matter to God. Listen to the way one mentor describes this responsibility:

> A spiritual mother [mentor] can't change the fact that a young woman's biological mother constantly criticizes her—but she can help that young woman see that her worth is in her identity as a daughter of the King.[3]

Mentors push us beyond the wounds, failures, and regrets of the past. The enemy wants to keep us bound in yesterday's bad memories, resurrecting forgiven sins and beating us over the head with them. Good mentors, though, recognize that fact and constantly remind us of God's forgiving grace. They don't allow us to live in yesterday's wrongs when salvation and today's victories are so powerful. Let your helmet of salvation be present tense.

What messages of the enemy most hinder your Christian walk?

How can a mentor help you stand firm against these messages?

The Sword of the Spirit

The sword of the Spirit is the Word of God—both a defensive and an offensive weapon. The Word is truth, and that truth exposes the enemy's lies. If you know the Word's teachings, claim its promises, and believe its truths, you can resist the devil (see James 4:7). He can't stand against God-breathed Scriptures (see 2 Timothy 3:16).

If the Word of God is so powerful, it's surprising that many believers don't read the Bible at all. You probably know some common excuses for not studying the Word (perhaps you've used them at some point): "I don't know where to begin." "I don't know how to read the Bible." "There are a lot of concepts and ideas I don't understand." "Sometimes it's boring." "I'm not sure it's relevant; the Bible was written a long time ago." "I've tried before, and I didn't get very far." "I don't have time."

Look at those excuses and consider ways many a mentor could help us. Mentors can teach us how to interpret and apply the Bible. They can show us why even the stories of the Bible that seem mundane can be exciting and relevant. From mentors we can learn principles of time management so that we have time for Bible reading. I've heard many excuses over the years, and I can't find any that a mentor couldn't address.

Ask God to give you a mentor to help you consistently read the Word. One strategy I've found effective as a mentor is to hold myself accountable to my mentees through daily reporting. At the beginning of every year, I adopt an annual reading strategy—usually one I find through an online search for "Bible-reading plans." Each day I read the passage, study it, pray about it, and send an email report to one of the people I mentor. The report is brief and simple:

- *Reading*. John 3
- *Insight gained*. Nicodemus came to Jesus at night. I don't know why he came at night; maybe he just wanted some private time with Jesus. Would I work so hard to be with Jesus?
- *Action steps*. Do whatever it takes to spend time with God and in His Word today.
- *Prayer*. Lord, I commit myself to be with You today. Help me.
- *Tomorrow's reading*. John 4

Writing this report takes only a few minutes, but it helps me stay faithful in my reading. In addition, it provides a journal of Bible reading for later reference. In fact, I now write an expanded devotion and post it on my website, www.chucklawless.com, for people who want to read the Word with me.

But there's more to the sword of the Spirit than reading the Word. The term translated *word* in the phrase "word of God" (v. 17) means not only to know the Word but also to speak it. That's a picture of mentoring: someone teaches us the Word, we obey it, and then we teach it to others. That's what it means to take up the sword of the Spirit.

Urgent Prayer

Prayer isn't a piece of the armor of God, but it's vital to living a strong Christian life. It was so important for Paul that he ended this passage on spiritual warfare with a focus on praying for one another. Notice his words of urgency:

 For strong Bible-reading plans, check out *Reader's Guide to the Bible* or *Foundations* at LifeWay.com.

Pray at all times in the Spirit with every prayer and request, and stay alert with all perseverance and intercession for all the saints (Ephesians 6:18).

"Every prayer," Paul said. "Pray at all times in the Spirit." "Stay alert." "All perseverance." "All the saints." Prayer matters.

Yet how often do most of us pray for one another? More specifically, when do we pray for one another? In most cases we don't pray for others until we hear about a problem. Seldom do we pray for one another just because we're brothers and sisters in Christ who are fighting a real spiritual battle. Frankly, we usually start praying only after someone has already lost a battle.

In response to this wrong understanding of prayer, we need mentors to teach us to pray as Jesus taught His disciples to pray—proactively and passionately (see Matthew 6:5-13).

Prayer is a discipline to learn, and opportunities to practice and model that discipline are everywhere. Think about ways mentors and mentees can practice prayer. If someone asks for prayer, pray right then. Pray when you hear a siren, see a hearse, or pass a car accident. Pray for churches as you drive or walk past their meeting places. As you watch the news, take time to pray for victims of war or natural disasters. Prayerwalk in a neighborhood, quietly praying for anyone you see. Pray for families and nations as you read the newspaper or a news website. Praise God in prayer when you hear of families restored, illness cured, and nonbelievers saved. Start and end your road trips with prayer. All types of prayer triggers can lead you to pray continually throughout the day.

At other times plan an intentional prayer strategy to focus on others. One of my mentees and I once walked through the streets of New York City praying for the people we passed. We talked very little as we walked. Instead, we looked, listened, and interceded. In that famous setting we saw the world. God had brought people from all over the globe—maybe just so that we could pray for them. Perhaps God intersected all of our lives that day.

More pointedly, I recognize that the enemy wants to defeat my mentees like Kevin, Nick, Mike, Chris, Daniel, Jason, and Kevin. He equally aims his arrows at the young women whom Pam is mentoring. If we're not praying for them before the enemy defeats them, we're not fulfilling our responsibility as mentors.

BE IN IT FOR THE LONG HAUL

Much of mentoring involves challenging people to do something—to take steps toward growth. The responsibilities of mentors are to guide their mentees, support them in their tasks, and encourage them toward progress in the Christian life. Mentors are what one resource has called " 'life ed' instructors"[4] who walk beside mentees and model Christian truth along the way.

The following ideas provide practical direction for your mentoring sessions. These make great discussion prompts.

Q & A Sessions

Mentoring is listening and telling; it's an exchange. Sometimes it's good to have intentional Q & A sessions. If you're a mentor, schedule lunch with your mentee and give him or her permission to ask anything. This approach can be risky for you because you never know what question might be asked, but it will help get in touch with the topics that matters to your mentee. Also, fresh topics might come up that you wouldn't have thought of otherwise.

Here are some of the questions I've been asked:

• How did you learn to develop your relationship with your non-Christian dad?
• I don't know how to do a budget. Where do I start?
• How did you know your wife was the one you were supposed to marry?
• What should I do if I want to drop out of school?
• How do I know God's will?
• What should my résumé format look like?
• How can I get experience when companies won't hire people without experience?
• What suggestions do you have for dealing with lust?
• What kind of lawnmower would you recommend?
• Do I need life insurance?
• What's your Bible-reading plan?
• Can you help me figure out a good way to surprise my spouse on her birthday?

The list could go on for several pages. Mentees typically love having someone to talk with about real issues, and this strategy makes that possible.

Case Studies

Most mentoring relationships provide enough real-life scenarios that mentors don't need hypothetical situations to discuss. In some situations, though, a case study is an effective means to start a dialogue. They're especially helpful in learning how to identify and examine different responses to a given situation. They can also you introduce and discuss values and issues so personal that a mentee might be afraid to bring them up.

Here are four case studies I've used to prompt discussions about Christian living.

Case 1. You're tired, but you still have two reports to complete for a class you're taking. You discover that you can order a paper on the Internet for less than twenty dollars, make some adjustments to make it sound like your writing, and turn it in for credit. What do you do?

Case 2. You recognize that you're developing lustful feelings for a coworker. What do you do to avoid falling into further sin? Do you tell your spouse about your feelings?

Case 3. Two months ago your bank wrongly applied four hundred dollars to your account, and you didn't catch it. At this point you've already spent most of the money. If you point out the bank's mistake, it will be corrected. If you stay quiet, you might not have to pay it back. What do you do?

Case 4. At the park you meet another mom who's a follower of a different world faith. You get to know her, and she seems godly and kind. Her kids love playing with your kids. You look forward to seeing her each day, and you don't want to offend her in any way. Do you tell her the good news of Jesus? If not, why not? If so, how?

The great thing about discussion starters like these is that you never know the direction the dialogue will take. The values you explore in talking about these decisions can elicit past stories and "Why I think this way" accounts, often teaching us what makes others tick.

Reading Lists

This option should begin with the people being mentored. Ask them what topics they would like to study; then work with them to create a reading list of books, Bible studies, websites, and online journals. A quick web search may show that the material is already available. Read the resources together and discuss them as you go.

What reading topics would most interest you?

What three books have been powerful influences in your life?

Interviews

One of my favorite mentoring roles is to facilitate interviews between people I mentor and people from whom they might learn. I've set up forty-five- to sixty-minute interviews with church pastors, CPAs, college deans, school principals, sales managers, physicians, missionaries, writers, politicians, and others. All of these people had more to teach than I did, and my role was only to make the interview possible. Most of the time I've learned as much as my mentees have. Now Skype and other technologies make interviews even more possible.

Whom would you most want to interview? Why?

How might a mentor help you with an interview?

Road Trips

If feasible, travel together as mentor and mentee. Time in a car can be some of the most focused, productive mentoring time. You can deal with a lot of life when your laptop is closed and your cell phone is muted. Even short trips can provide opportunities to talk and learn.

I encourage mentors to adopt this rule as much as possible: don't travel alone. If you always have someone with you, you model practical accountability while also providing opportunities for that person to learn. Take one of the people you mentor on a business trip and stop at historic sites along the route. Ask your mentee to do some research prior to the trip. Then review lessons learned at those sites. Set up interviews with church leaders in the area. Plan at least one activity that's just relaxing and fun. Pray as you go.

START ON THE WAY TOGETHER

These suggestions are tools that can help you and your mentor or mentee blend your lives together. The mentoring relationship is more than two people walking parallel paths. It's two people walking the same path and sharing their lives along the way. You can spend time with someone, even studying the Bible, and still be functioning at a head level rather than a heart level. It's not until we share our lives that our interactions become investments in each other and we bond as brothers and sisters in Christ.

Just as essential as the gear that helps us engage in spiritual battle is the camaraderie we develop with our fellow soldiers. As we trust, listen, and learn from each other, together we'll grow to be more like Jesus.

For a list of historic sites worth visiting, check out the National Register of Historic Places at nps.gov.

THROUGH THE WEEK

> STUDY: Begin a plan of action to put on the full armor of God daily.

> PRAY: Ask God to help you become deeply invested in the Word of God through reading, studying, and listening. Every piece of the armor of God is connected to the Word.

> CONNECT: Make a list of the people in your life who wear the armor of God well. Ask them to describe their strategies for staying spiritually protected. Begin modeling their tactics in your life.

> A SUGGESTION FOR MENTORS: Recognizing that you're a target for the enemy, make sure you have prayer partners who regularly intercede for you as you mentor.

> A SUGGESTION FOR MENTEES: Pray daily for your mentor. He or she is in the enemy's sights.

1. Chuck Lawless, *Discipled Warriors* (Grand Rapids, MI: Kregel, 2003), 43–44.
2. Michael Card, *The Walk* (Nashville: Thomas Nelson, 2000), Kindle edition, location 166.
3. Susan Hunt, *Spiritual Mothering* (Wheaton, IL: Crossway, 1992), Kindle edition, location 149.
4. Bo Boshers and Judson Poling, *The Be-with Factor* (Grand Rapids, MI: Zondervan, 2006), Kindle edition, location 1609.

SESSION SIX

PREPARING FOR POTHOLES AND POSSIBILITIES

I travel a lot, both by plane and by car. When you travel as much as I do, you expect to encounter obstacles and difficulties somewhere on the journey. The flight with the picturesque takeoff hits serious turbulence in the middle of the flight. Some international roadways aren't well maintained, with decaying asphalt, disappearing shoulders, and widening potholes. Security agents in airports and police officers directing traffic are working for the good of society, but they sometimes slow the process. Sometimes the along-the-way journey can become tedious and frustrating.

Mentoring can be equally frustrating at times. Some mentees who no longer want to be involved suddenly disappear without explanation. In other cases the relationship itself doesn't work. I remember a mentee who sought me out, and I began meeting with him. About two months into our meetings, I realized that the relationship wouldn't last long. He missed meetings and always had elaborate excuses. When we met, his arrogance frustrated me. He expected attention but wanted no expectations to be placed on him. We met until our six-month evaluation time, and I chose to end the relationship.

Problems like these can be avoided if we're aware of the early-warning signs. Let's look at some of those signs and then consider the potential life transformation that mentoring offers.

POTENTIAL POTHOLES
I spent most of my life in the Midwest, where winter storms are common. Snow and ice build up on the roads, and the freezing-thawing process produces potholes galore. I've seen holes so large that I thought I would lose the front end of my car if I didn't stay alert. In fact, my cars frequently needed front-end alignments because of potholes.

I wish the potholes of mentoring were always so obvious. As you start mentoring, be alert for problems that might hinder your progress. Here are a few.

Pothole: Failing to Establish Expectations

As I mentioned before, at the outset of a new mentoring relationship, I ask my potential mentee to write his "The sky's the limit" list of hopes and expectations for the relationship. After that we negotiate our mutual expectations. I want us both to know up front what we want to accomplish so that we're aiming in the same direction.

Jesus took this approach with His followers. People knew what He demanded of them before they decided to follow Him. His expectations were heavy but undeniably clear. His followers didn't always understand His teachings, but none of them could say they didn't know what He expected. Listen to a few of his demands:

> Jesus said to his disciples, "If anyone wants to follow after me, let him deny himself, take up his cross, and follow me" (Matthew 16:24).

> "Follow me," Jesus told them, "and I will make you fish for people" (Mark 1:17).

> Jesus said to him, "No one who puts his hand to the plow and looks back is fit for the kingdom of God" (Luke 9:62).

Unless you repent, you will all perish as well (Luke 13:3).

If anyone comes to me and does not hate his own father and mother, wife and children, brothers and sisters—yes, and even his own life—he cannot be my disciple (Luke 14:26).

It was clear that Jesus expected a commitment from His followers. In a mentoring relationship, stating mutual expectations at the beginning lessens the possibility that somebody will be disappointed at the end. I wish I had understood this reality years ago when working with a mentee, Chris, before I began requiring "The sky's the limit" document. I assumed he primarily wanted to grow as a Christian, and he assumed he would gain some benefits by being a mentee of the seminary dean. Somehow Chris never stated his expectations, and I didn't quickly pick up on signals he was sending. By the time I figured out what was happening, Chris was already disappointed with our relationship. The mentoring ended, and I learned a valuable lesson from the situation.

How would you describe the difficulties of dealing with unmet expectations in a relationship?

What would be your top three expectations for a productive mentoring relationship?

Pothole: Tutoring Rather than Mentoring

A tutor's job is to give individual attention that helps you learn or improve in an area of weakness. A student's role is to listen, ask questions, and learn. Tutoring is information-centered more than life-centered.

Of course, mentoring sometimes includes teaching information. At times the mentee just listens and learns, but a mentor's role isn't simply giving answers. He or she should help a mentee figure out an answer. It's the difference in the old adage between giving a hungry man a fish and teaching him how to fish. Teach him how to fish, and he will get his own meals in the future and teach others to do the same. Mentoring should lead to independence from the mentor and dependence on God.

Learning to mentor rather than tutor means learning to listen well. Good mentors don't jump ahead to the answer; they listen to the person being mentored, respond as needed, and point to solutions. They've learned how to read and hear their mentees through good listening practices like the following.

- Beginning the conversation with prayer that asks God to help you listen
- Giving the mentee undivided attention
- Watching body language while listening (for example, fidgeting, avoiding eye contact, nodding)
- Trying not to interrupt when the mentee is speaking
- Asking for clarification if something is unclear
- Summarizing major issues to verify understanding
- Asking for permission before giving advice (for example, say, "You know, I think there's another option. Mind if I tell you about it?")
- Making sure next steps are clearly understood
- Ending the time with prayer that asks God to help you appropriately follow up on the conversation.

Here's an example of mentoring more than tutoring. One of my mentees, Jonathan, wanted to know more about doctoral programs. The easiest thing for me to do would have been to tell him all I know about those options since I live in the world of doctoral studies every day. Because I've learned the hard way not to give all the answers, though, I first told him to learn what he could on his own through a web search. He did that, and my job was only to provide clarity and answer questions. Jonathan now knows more than I would have told him, and he's even prepared to help guide others who ask the same question. We successfully avoided the pothole in that situation.

Are you more comfortable in a tutoring role or a mentoring role? Why?

Who's the best listener you know? What makes him or her a good listener?

Pothole: Refusing to Confront

Although a mentor needs to listen well, he or she must also be willing to confront a mentee if the situation warrants it. To do anything less is uncaring. The Bible demands that we be willing to confront one another when our lives are marred by sin. These Scripture verses issue a clear call to accountability and confrontation:

> **If your brother sins against you, go and rebuke him in private. If he listens to you, you have won your brother. But if he won't listen, take one or two others with you, so that by the testimony of two or three witnesses every fact may be established (Matthew 18:15-16).**

 "Effective mentors stick with helping, not interfering. They share, they model, they teach; they do not take over someone else's problems unless there is a crisis that requires immediate action."—Gordon Shea, *Mentoring*[1]

Brothers and sisters, if someone is overtaken in any wrongdoing, you who are spiritual, restore such a person with a gentle spirit, watching out for yourselves so that you also won't be tempted (Galatians 6:1).

Obey your leaders and submit to them, since they keep watch over your souls as those who will give an account, so that they can do this with joy and not with grief, for that would be unprofitable for you (Hebrews 13:17).

If the Bible is so clear, why don't we confront as needed? Maybe we're concerned that confrontation will cost too much: we might lose a friendship, someone might get angry, or we don't want to create a difficult situation for ourselves or anyone else. Many people have never been taught how to confront in a healthy way. Some of us have poor histories with confrontation. We would rather avoid the possible conflict than go through that again.

Not only does avoiding confrontation fail to solve anything, but it also makes us disobedient to the Word that demands we speak the truth in love to others (see Ephesians 4:15). Because confrontation is both difficult and necessary, we must "build bridges of relationship that can bear the weight of truth."[2] Mentor and mentee must trust each other—and more specifically, trust God who brought them together in a divine intersection—enough to speak and hear painful truths.

Again, this is why mentoring is so powerful. No one wants to be confronted, but we would prefer to be confronted by a friend if confrontation is warranted. I would rather have a friend speak truth to me any day because I know that person speaks from love. Mentors who genuinely care will help their mentees face reality, even when it hurts. The wounds of a friend are trustworthy (see Proverbs 27:6).

Can you remember the last time someone confronted you about your spiritual life? What feelings did his or her words stir in you?

How do you typically respond when confronted?

Pothole: Developing Jealousy

Jealousy is a monster that can consume us all. We mentors sometimes struggle with our own egos when mentees surpass us in an area. As much as we want to respond differently, our self-centeredness becomes apparent when someone we know grows beyond us and is recognized accordingly.

Mentees can also become jealous of one another. The Gospel of Mark tells the story of a distraught father who brought his demon-possessed son to Jesus' disciples (see Mark 9:14-37). Under the demon's influence the boy couldn't speak, foamed at the mouth, and often threw himself into fire or water to destroy himself. From his childhood he had been in this condition, and nothing had changed. In desperation the man brought his son to Jesus' disciples. Later, speaking to Jesus, he described the situation this way:

> **I asked your disciples to drive it out, but they couldn't (Mark 9:18).**

"But they couldn't." God's power was available to the disciples, but they somehow missed it. In the following verses we learn that the disciples' failure was a product of faithlessness (see v. 19) and prayerlessness (see v. 29).

Sometime later Jesus retreated with His disciples and taught them about His coming betrayal, death, and resurrection, but the disciples didn't fully understand what He was teaching (see vv. 30-32). What's even more disconcerting, however, is that in the very next passage these same disciples were debating over who was the greatest:

> **When he was in the house, he asked them, "What were you arguing about on the way?" But they were silent, because on the way they had been arguing with one another about who was the greatest (Mark 9:33-34).**

Cast out a demon? They couldn't do it. Comprehend Jesus' teaching about His death? They failed. Understand the nature of Jesus' kingdom? Not yet. Willingly follow Christ's model of service? Not even close. Yet these men were arguing over who was the greatest in a kingdom they didn't even understand.

Later the disciples' pettiness was evident again when they tried to shut down someone else who was exorcising demons, simply because he wasn't one of them (see v. 38). They also became angry and envious because a mother sought the best seats in God's kingdom for her sons (see Matthew 20:20-28). Even though the disciples at times failed in ministry, they remained arrogant enough to be jealous and petty on occasion.

Let's not kid ourselves, though. We can be the same way at times. We notice when a mentor or church-staff member spends more time with someone else than with us. We wonder why they seem to have favorites. The kind of pettiness and jealousy we see among the disciples, we can observe in ourselves. And the result is the same for both— anger and broken relationships.

Pothole: Surrendering to Spiritual Letdown

Picture this. A group of guys gathers weekly to hold one another accountable about pornography, with the goals of fighting for holiness and pleasing God with their lives. The first week the men who've failed are broken over their sin. They don't usually cry in public, but they do this night. The second week they admit their struggles but are less emotional about them. The third week they hold back a bit, more concerned about measuring up in the group. About the fourth week of their accountability group, Jeremy admits his failure in a joking manner. The others laugh with him, although uncomfortably. When Pete admits failure too, the laughing comes a bit easier.

By the tenth week almost all of the men have admitted falling into sin again. Nobody weeps now, however, as he confesses his wrong. In fact, the men almost assume that most of them will have failed during the previous week. They don't say it aloud, but they've given one another permission to fail by their decreasing conviction over their sin.

That's spiritual letdown—dropping your guard about sin so that it becomes easier and easier to give in to temptation. It often occurs in groups, but it also occurs between mentor and mentee. Because confession is difficult and strong relationships are rare, we sometimes let each other off the hook from keeping spiritual commitments. "At least you're doing better than you used to," we say. "Well, I'm not perfect either, so let's not worry about it this time." Decreasing sensitivity leads to increasing permission to fail.

In many ways this same danger is inherent in good mentoring. Mentoring demands sharing along-the-way time, and time spent together opens the door to seeing each other's faults. The more time you spend with a person, the more likely you'll see his or her sin. When that time comes, beware of any tendency to let down spiritually. Rigorously continue to hold each other accountable.

Pothole: Choosing Not to Multiply

If you read enough works on mentoring, you'll read more than one description of the stages of a mentoring relationship. However, most include the assumption that mentoring will lead to the mentee's investing in someone else's life. Consider the following stages of mentoring.

Stages of Mentoring

Definition. The relationship is introduced and defined.
Development. Longest and often most productive component of the relationship; the growth and development of the mentee
Departure. Ideally, the mentee becomes an equal and mentors someone else.[3]

 "The true test of relationships is not only how loyal we are when friends fail, but how thrilled we are when they succeed."
—John Maxwell, *Mentoring 101*[4]

Here's another way to think of these stages:

Initiation. Getting to know each other; the mentee is excited and anxious.
Cultivation. The mentee grows in confidence and competence.
Separation. The mentee is less dependent on the mentor; the mentee becomes a colleague.
Redefinition. There's less frequent contact as the mentoring relationship ends.

Or:

Come and see. The first encounter to get to know each other
Come and follow. Commitment to the expectations of mentoring
Come and surrender. Deep commitment to the mentor and the mentor's cause
Come and multiply. The mentee now invests in others.

Whatever you call it, the final stage of effective mentoring results in a new mentor-mentee relationship as the mentee becomes the mentor. The first-generation mentoring relationship really isn't complete until a second-generation relationship is established. It's a problem when this next-generation connection never gets started.

Why doesn't multiplication happen? Sometimes it's because the mentor doesn't want to let go of the relationship with the mentee. Mentors receive affirmation when mentees respect and learn from them. That affirmation is often so powerful that mentors don't want to lose it.

Multiplication can also be thwarted when mentees don't want to move on. They often feel affirmed because someone gives them attention and time. Sometimes it's more comfortable to stay in the receiving role than to take responsibility for training someone else. Receiving attention is almost always easier than giving attention.

In other cases mentees simply haven't been challenged to invest in someone else. They might make the investment if they knew it was an essential part of the process, but their mentors never stated the expectation clearly, didn't encourage them to start the next cycle, or didn't equip them to reach out to someone else.

Sometimes the mentee doesn't want to pay the cost of mentoring. What if he or she fails as a mentor? What if he or she doesn't have the time to give and the willingness to sacrifice? What if he or she doesn't have the discipline it takes to stay ahead of the next-generation mentee? If any of these situations prevent a mentee from becoming a mentor, a significant step in the mentoring process remains missing.

One solution to this problem is for a mentor to talk about this eventual goal early in the relationship. All of us can find someone to mentor in our workplace, university,

For a glimpse into a mentoring relationship in action, watch video session 6, "Jason and Dakota's Story," available at lifeway.com/mentor.

or church. I encourage my mentees to find that person within the first three months of our mentoring relationship. That way I can serve as a sounding board and resource person for my mentee as he moves toward investing in the next generation.

What are some other hesitations about mentoring that you've experienced?

What factors would (or did) daunt you about becoming a mentor?

POTENTIAL POSSIBILITIES

We've discussed potholes in mentoring—challenges that can run us off the road—but the potholes don't have to outweigh the possibilities. Being a part of a mentoring relationship is an investment, both in another person and in yourself. Nothing good, no real investment, comes without its costs and challenges. But a good investment also comes with a return. Here are some of the greatest possibilities from or returns on the investment of mentoring and being mentored.

Possibility: Finding Authentic, Rich Relationships

You should recognize by now that divine intersections are the supernatural connections God makes between people, as He did with Paul and Timothy. We may not realize the miracle of this kind of connection when it happens, but the gift of a person changes our lives. It's more than simple similarity or common values. It's something that happens at a deeper level than the words we say to each other. At times these relationships don't even require words; it's the presence of the person who meets us and teaches us that's so meaningful and life-changing.

I've learned about that kind of depth in a few mentoring relationships. Kevin and I have that kind of bond. He and I have driven many miles and hiked many hours through Kentucky and North Carolina woods, often with only necessary words between us. Both of us like quiet, and somehow our relationship is strengthened in that silence. It's strange, actually—we've learned to trust each other as brothers in Christ without talking much. Even now I visit him where he serves the Lord in Mexico, and silence is OK despite the many months between our visits. There's a comfort in that kind of bond.

With other mentoring relationships, talking is much more the norm. Chris always has questions for me, and he and I have talked into the early hours of the morning many times. I know when we meet, we're going to enter deep discussions. My wife, Pam, knows that several of her mentees will come to lunch with life questions on their minds.

Understanding God's direction and navigating relationships are almost always topics of discussion. That's OK, though, because God has given us this opportunity to walk together with others along the way.

What are some signs for you that a relationship has gone to a deep, authentic level?

What experiences do you share with people that seem to take the relationships to deeper places?

Possibility: Expanding Your Influence

The movie *Mr. Holland's Opus* is the story of Glenn Holland, a musician who longs to compose his own music. Holland turns to teaching to make extra money, and that teaching becomes his livelihood after his wife gives birth to a deaf son. Thirty years later the principal of Holland's school ends the music program due to budget cuts. As Holland leaves the building for the last time, he finds students from his many years of teaching who've gathered to sing and play in his honor. A former student speaks about the power of Mr. Holland as a mentor:

> Mr. Holland had a profound influence on my life and on a lot of lives I know. But I have a feeling that he considers a great part of his own life misspent. Rumor had it he was always working on this symphony of his. And this was going to make him famous, rich, probably both. But Mr. Holland isn't rich and he isn't famous, at least not outside of our little town. So it might be easy for him to think himself a failure. But he would be wrong, because I think that he's achieved a success far beyond riches and fame. Look around you. There is not a life in this room that you have not touched, and each of us is a better person because of you. We are your symphony, Mr. Holland. We are the melodies and the notes of your opus. We are the music of your life.[5]

As a teacher, I find those words powerful and moving because that's what I want to do: to touch lives. And I want to do this for God's glory so that believers become better followers of Christ. Mentoring gives me that opportunity. In fact, I'm humbled when I think of what God is doing through many of my mentees over the years. I'm so proud of these men and so grateful to God for the privilege of mentoring them:

- A missionary in Asia
- A successful manager at Chick-fil-A
- A missionary in East Asia
- A church planter in the Pacific Rim
- A denominational leader in Ohio
- A businessman in Illinois
- A church-staff member in Florida
- A pastor in New York City
- A pastor in Alabama
- A church planter in Denver
- An insurance agent in Kentucky
- A missionary in Africa
- A missionary leader in the Americas
- A college minister in Louisiana
- A professor in Malaysia

When I think of these men and others, I thank God for them. I thank God for the families many of them now lead. And I clearly remember that I've been privileged to mentor them because somebody else first invested in me. Somebody influenced me along the way so that I can influence others.

What names are on your list of mentees, formal and informal, through the years?

In what ways do you feel different now about mentoring than you did when you were younger?

Possibility: Appreciating and Offering Grace

Nobody's perfect, and everybody will fail somewhere along the way. As a good mentor, you'll anguish over that failure, sometimes more than your mentee will. You'll grieve on your knees when your mentee makes poor choices that lead to trouble.

But the good news is that God is the God of second chances. Think about Simon Peter, one of Jesus' primary mentees, who miserably failed when he denied knowing Jesus (see Luke 22:31-61). Watch the steps to Peter's collapse in denying Christ:

1. *Overconfidence (see vv. 31-34).* Peter was overly confident in his own faithfulness to Jesus. In the same way, our confidence can cloud the reality that all of us have the potential of denying Christ before the rooster crows in the morning.

2. *Emotional and physical fatigue (see vv. 39-46).* Emotional drain, physical weariness, and spiritual confusion caused Peter and the other disciples to sleep when they should have been praying.

3. *Prayerlessness (see vv. 45-46)*. Jesus asked the disciples to pray, but they didn't. Overconfidence + fatigue + prayerlessness is almost always a recipe for spiritual disaster.

4. *Self-reliance (see vv. 47-53)*. Mistaken confidence in our own power leads to our trying to solve problems in our own way. That's what Peter did when he took out his sword.

5. *Recklessness (see vv. 54-55)*. Peter found himself sitting in the wrong place with the wrong people at the wrong time. There was a reason that happened—carelessness. Just like Peter, we often find ourselves in the wrong place at the wrong time because we trust in ourselves and let our guard down.

6. *Self-protection (see vv. 56-60)*. Peter, by his words and actions, denied knowing Jesus three times. Frightened, defensive, and spiritually vulnerable, Peter fell. We can find ourselves in a similar state every day.

Just as Jesus had warned, the rooster crowed (see v. 60). Look closely, though, at the picture in verse 61: "The Lord turned and looked at Peter." Those words ought to cause us to stop reading and think about that scenario.

Jesus was under arrest, heading toward a cross. Peter attempted to blend in with the enemies, even verbally denying his commitment to Christ. The disciple who had said he would die for his mentor was unwilling even to admit his relationship with Him. In the midst of Peter's denials, the Lord Himself turned and looked at Peter. Face to face. Eyeball to eyeball. Heart to heart. Loving Lord to denying disciple. Mentor to mentee. The moment must have been agonizing for the mentee, who had just done what he said he would never do. All he could do now was weep like a baby.

The story doesn't end there, though. On resurrection morning an angel met the women at the tomb and told them to tell the good news to Jesus' disciples and Peter (see Mark 16:7)—as if to say, "Don't forget that Peter is still one of them too." His fall didn't ultimately break his relationship with Jesus; the Lord whom Peter denied wouldn't deny him. Indeed, Jesus would later affirm Peter as a shepherd set apart to feed His sheep (see John 21:15-17). What amazing grace is evident when a fallen fisherman is not only restored but also set apart to lead in God's kingdom!

We get the privilege to offer that same grace to our fallen mentees too. In mentoring we have a unique opportunity to model Christ's love—and to receive it.

As you review the steps to Peter's denial, which of these steps threaten your spiritual walk the most?

 Would you believe that mentoring affects the brain of the mentee? A study at Case Western Reserve University has shown that positive mentoring causes changes in the area of the brain that processes visual information.

Describe the difficulties of extending grace to yourself or someone else who has failed in his or her spiritual goals.

Possibility: Receiving Blessings and Prayers

To put it simply, mentoring brings a lot of blessings. I could never list all the blessings I've received, but here's a start. As a mentor, I've been blessed by men who pray for me and love me, "grandchildren" who call me Papaw Chuck, Father's Day cards and texts from around the world, young men who become faithful husbands and loving fathers, and Skype conversations with followers of Christ who serve among the nations.

As a mentee, I've been blessed with men who are always available when I need advice. They love me, pray for me, and encourage me. When I've struggled, my mentors have stood beside me and prayed me through the battles. They've directed me toward opportunities and challenged me to push myself beyond my level of comfort. All have loved and welcomed my wife. I suspect that I wouldn't be where I am today without my mentors, and they've truly been God's blessings to me.

However, my mentors have blessed me in another way. They've granted me forgiveness when needed, directed me when I've been confused, and loved me when I've messed up. They've shown me grace I didn't deserve.

As a young child, I learned about grace in a most unexpected way—watching professional wrestling with my grandma. "Rasslin'," she called it. We gathered around her television many Saturdays to watch her heroes.

Occasionally those heroes became bad guys and joined the villain teams in the ring. I would have thought this shift in loyalties might disgust my grandma and we would stop watching the show. That didn't happen, though. Instead, my grandma always believed her heroes would come back; they would eventually return to the good side. Just the possibility of their return gave my grandma hope. So that we wouldn't miss the fulfillment of her faith, we kept watching rasslin' until her hero-turned-villain became a good guy again.

Grandma always saw the good in her heroes, even when they turned evil. Give them enough time, and they would come back into the good-guy fold. "You can't give up on them," she would say. "Good will come from this."

There have been times in my life when I've needed to hear my grandma's words on my behalf: "You can't give up on him." In those times God has sent one mentor after another who've never given up on me. It's hard to find that kind of blessing.

Think of someone who has believed in you. How did that person's faith in you affect your life?

What makes us keep believing in someone when he or she seems to have fallen off the right path?

A FINAL CHALLENGE FOR YOU

I've mentioned throughout this study my trips down the Ocoee River with some of my mentees. Now let me tell you the rest of the story. Twice I've begun that journey, and twice we pulled our raft from the river before completing the trip. For various reasons I've not yet made it completely down the river. That challenge is still before me, though, and I'm looking forward to conquering it somewhere along the way in my journey. I suspect that one of my mentees will be with me, and we'll complete the trip together.

I don't know what journey God has planned for your life, and I can't know what rapids you might encounter on the way. But I know He expects someone to help you grow in your Christian faith. He wants other believers to disciple you, to walk with you along the way as you become more Christlike.

Maybe God's plan is for you to be the best engineer in the world or the most knowledgeable physician or nurse. Or perhaps the most talented singer or musician or the most gifted teacher in any school. A great salesman. A skilled writer. A courageous police officer. Whatever God wants for you, He expects you to grow along the way. A good mentor will help you get there.

Or perhaps God is calling you to vocational ministry. Maybe He wants you to be a pastor or a missionary. A denominational leader. A seminary or university professor. A church planter. A worship leader. A church-staff member. If God is calling you, He also has someone ready to mentor you. Take heart in that truth.

Somebody is waiting to disciple you along the way. Be patient but persistent as you pray to find this person. Then go, walk in his or her shadow, and discover the power of God. Finally, in that power invest yourself in someone else.

Thanks for walking along this path with me through this Bible study.

THROUGH THE WEEK

> PRAY: Pray that God will protect your heart and mind from spiritual letdown in your mentoring relationships.

> WATCH: For a challenging and inspiring look at the impact of investing in someone's life, check out the classic film *The Karate Kid*.

> CONNECT: Plan to start meeting with a potential mentor or mentee this month and begin applying what you've learned in this study.

> A SUGGESTION FOR MENTORS: Regularly send thank-you notes, emails, or texts to men and women who've invited you to invest in their lives. Mentees sometimes make a bigger commitment than we do in this process.

> A SUGGESTION FOR MENTEES: Get in the practice of setting goals for your continued spiritual growth. Based on this study, write three or four goals you want to accomplish in the next six months. Share them with your mentor and with someone you're mentoring.

1. Gordon F. Shea, *Mentoring* (Boston: Thomson, 2002), 65.
2. Tim Elmore, *Lifegiving Mentors* (Nashville: Thomas Nelson, 2000), Kindle edition, location 1459.
3. See Howard and William Hendricks, *As Iron Sharpens Iron* (Chicago: Moody, 1995), Kindle edition, 218–19; W. Brad Johnson and Charles R. Ridley, *The Elements of Mentoring* (New York: Palgrave McMillan, 2004), 126–30; Elmore, *Lifegiving Mentors*, Kindle edition, location 1022–67.
4. John Maxwell, *Mentoring 101* (Nashville: Thomas Nelson, 2008), Kindle edition, location 670.
5. "Mr. Holland's Opus Quotes," cited June 16, 2011, www.quotes.net.

MENTOR

LEADER GUIDE

WELCOME to the *Mentor* leader guide. This leader guide is designed to provide you, the leader, with the foundation you need to lead your group through an effective, engaging, and meaningful Bible study. As the group leader, you have the unique responsibility to set the tone for your group and to guide each session's conversation. As you spend time with your group members, pray with them and serve them in unexpected ways. When you lay a foundation of trust and belonging, you invite God to transform the lives of your group members.

LEADER TOOLS

Additional leader tools are provided to help you lead your group at lifeway.com/mentor.

> *Mentor* promotional video
> Seven video sessions that profile a variety of real-life mentoring relationships
>> Introduction: "Chuck Lawless on Mentoring"
>> Session 1: "Jason and Jordan's Story"
>> Session 2: "Leigh Ann and Heather's Story"
>> Session 3: "Dave, Teddy, and Patrick's Story"
>> Session 4: "Carrie and Courtney's Story"
>> Session 5: "Arliss and Linda's Story"
>> Session 6: "Jason and Dakota's Story"
> Visual aids that can be adapted for your group or church's use, including a promotional poster, church bulletin insert, and PowerPoint® slides.

You'll also find study notes, commentaries, articles, word studies, and other resources to supplement your preparation at mywsb.com.

QUESTIONS AND DISCUSSION

This leader guide provides key questions to help facilitate group discussion. You'll notice that the leader guide offers four specific points of action for you as a leader:

ENGAGE: Introductory questions that everyone can easily answer. These help break the ice and get the conversation started.

ENCOUNTER: Focus on God's Word and one another. These questions ask what the biblical text says or means about a particular topic.

EXPRESS: Ask, "So what?" Identify ways truth applies directly to our lives.

EQUIP: Parting thoughts to leave your group with. Includes a creative prayer element that will reemphasize the principles from the session.

SESSION 1
Understanding Along-the-Way Discipleship

ENGAGE

Here's my favorite definition of *mentoring:* "A God-given relationship in which one growing Christian encourages and equips another believer to reach his or her potential as a disciple of Christ."[1] (p. 10).

> Which words in that definition stand out as key words for understanding mentoring?

> Think about the people who've been the most powerful influences in your spiritual walk. In what ways does this definition describe their roles in your life?

Watch video session 1, "Jason and Jordan's Story."

> What stands out to you from Jason's and Jordan's comments about their mentoring relationship?

> Which defining characteristics of mentoring, as stated in the previous definition, do you see modeled by Jason and Jordan?

In the video Jason makes the following statement: "When you consider the goal of mentoring, it's really closely connected to discipleship. For me personally, those things really can't be separated. … Discipleship at its core is something that passes fame and reknown of God from one generation to the next."

> Do you agree with Jason's statement? Why or why not?

> What are some benefits of making mentoring a key aspect of discipleship?

ENCOUNTER

"The goal of Christian mentoring is that the mentor lives like Jesus, the disciple becomes more and more like Jesus, and both continue to lead others to do the same. It's hard to find a loftier goal than becoming like Jesus. Mentoring matters in an eternal way" (p. 14).

> What words would you use to describe someone who's becoming more like Jesus?

> In what ways can someone be guided to become more like Jesus? What does that process look like from your experience?

> Brother Jack was someone who taught by the way he lived even more than the words he spoke. Describe someone in your life who had the kind of influence Brother Jack did.

Read 1 Corinthians 11:1.
Imitate me, as I also imitate Christ.

> That's a pretty bold statement for anyone to make: if you become like me, then you'll become more like Jesus. But that's the essence of mentoring. How does humility complement that statement?

> How would you complete the sentence "You'll become more like Jesus as you do these things like me: …"?

> Both equipping and encouraging are essential elements to a mentoring relationship. In what ways does this verse encompass both?

Read 2 Timothy 2:2.
What you have heard from me in the presence of many witnesses, commit to faithful men who will be able to teach others also.

> Mentoring isn't simply teaching, yet it includes a teaching element. As you think about passing on your faith to someone as this verse describes, what methods would be involved?

> This verse describes a kind of mentor sandwich—to be mentored by someone and to mentor someone else at the same time. How do you respond to that idea in terms of schedule and time frame?

EXPRESS
"You don't always have to be older than people to be their mentor. Even younger believers can be mentors as long as they're being discipled. Investing in others requires only that you're one step ahead in some area—that you've learned something you can give to others. Whatever your age, life experience and Christian growth make the most effective tools for mentors" (p. 18).

> In what ways have your life experiences prepared you to help someone else?

> In what areas do you have the most to offer in terms of Christian growth?

> If comfortable, describe a mistake you've made that now gives you a platform from which to advise others.

EQUIP
Direct the group to pray silently. First have members pray for the person on their left, then for the person on their right. Then have them pray for someone who's an influence in their lives, then someone they're trying to influence. Close in prayer together, asking God to open your eyes to see the opportunities He offers to participate in mentoring relationships.

---

1. Chuck Lawless, *Making Disciples through Mentoring* (Forest, VA, and Elkton, MD: Church Growth Institute, 2002), 14.

SESSION 2
Learning from the Master: Jesus & His Disciples

ENGAGE
"There are many ways, in Christ's name, we can give up our lives for those who follow us, such as the choices we make to be the kind of person they need to follow, the time we give them, and the opportunities we turn down. These are godly sacrifices, made as we invest ourselves in others to help them become more like Jesus" (p. 34).

> Describe the kinds of sacrifices a person would typically make to be in a mentoring relationship.

> What do you think it was like to be a disciple of Jesus?

Watch video session 2, "Leigh Ann and Heather's Story."

> What stands out to you from Leigh Ann's and Heather's comments about their mentoring relationship?

> Which aspects of Jesus' disciple-making model in session 2 are evident in Leigh Ann and Heather's story?

ENCOUNTER
"Jesus, in His authority as the Son of God, ordered us to make disciples by sharing the gospel and teaching believers. Then He assured us of the power to get the job done. … How do we tap into this power that's promised in Scripture so that it's evident in our mentoring relationships? First, we admit we can't make disciples on our own" (p. 35).

> What roles do you find, both inside and outside the church, that reflect a discipleship mentality through which people pass on what they have learned (for example, apprenticeships, internships, etc.)?

Read 2 Thessalonians 1:11-12.
In view of this, we always pray for you that our God will make you worthy of his calling, and by his power fulfill your every desire to do good and your work produced by faith, so that the name of our Lord Jesus will be glorified by you, and you by him, according to the grace of our God and the Lord Jesus Christ.

> What words would you use to describe our purpose as people who follow God?

> In what ways can a mentor help someone discover his or her purpose?

Read Mark 3:14.
He appointed twelve, whom he also named apostles, to be with Him, to send them out to preach.

> Part of what Jesus called the Twelve to do is simply to be with Him. What priority did Jesus place on hanging out with the disciples as one of His discipling methods?

> Jesus spent time with His disciples, and He gave them jobs to do. These assignments required accountability about whether they had completed their tasks. What makes accountability a difficult topic in a mentoring relationship?

Read Jude 24-25.

Now to him who is able to protect you from stumbling and to make you stand in the presence of his glory, without blemish and with great joy, to the only God our Savior, through Jesus Christ our Lord, be glory, majesty, power, and authority before all time, now and forever. Amen.

> Along with His presence and direction, Jesus gave His followers the power and authority to do what He asked them to. Are there any areas in which you lack confidence that you have the power to do what God wants you to do in the lives of others? What would help you feel that power and authority in your life?

EXPRESS

"It's God's responsibility to empower and grow the people you mentor. At the end of the day, you're responsible to remain faithful to your task and to do what Jesus did" (p. 38).

> What do you see as the most difficult task in mentoring?

> What kinds of things can we do or resources can we consult to find patience and persistence to continue working with someone who's difficult?

EQUIP

As a group, create a list of desirable qualities someone needs to influence others to be more like Jesus. Lead the group in a responsive prayer. Pray about each item on the list, saying, "God give us _____" as the group responds, "Make us like Jesus." When you've prayed through the whole list, close the prayer.

SESSION 3
Mentoring in Action: Paul & Timothy

ENGAGE

"Not even the best mentors come close to perfect. Mentors are often just one step ahead of their disciples. In Paul's case he had many leadership qualities, but his background was far from what you would expect for a Christian mentor" (p. 43).

> We all have mistakes in our pasts, situations we would love to do over. What words would you use to describe the feeling of having something in your past that you're not proud of?

> How can we keep our pasts from limiting what we have to offer another person in a mentoring relationship?

ENCOUNTER

"If perfection and a spiritual pedigree were requirements for mentors, none of us would have or be one. Many mentors are effective precisely because they've navigated tough situations in their lives. Because they've overcome their own regrettable decisions, they can lead others to do the same. Some of the best mentors I know have a deep appreciation for God's forgiving grace because they've experienced it so deeply. They've conquered their pasts through the power of God" (p. 43).

> Describe a time when a mistake in your past prepared you for something you faced in life.

> Is it easy for you to get distracted by someone's faults or mistakes when you want to learn from them? What are some strategies to keep that from happening?

Read 2 Corinthians 12:9.
He said to me, "My grace is sufficient for you, for my power is perfected in weakness." Therefore, I will most gladly boast all the more about my weaknesses, so that Christ's power may reside in me.

> Our culture places a high value on independence and self-confidence. How can we reconcile those values with God's desire to work in our weaknesses?

> If you're mentoring someone, how can boasting about your weaknesses encourage that person to grow? If you're being mentored, can you describe some experiences in which you've learned from your mentor's vulnerability about his or her weaknesses?

> What's the difference between boasting in your weaknesses through which God's power is shown and taking glory in your weaknesses?

Read 1 Timothy 1:12-16.
I give thanks to Christ Jesus our Lord who has strengthened me, because he considered me faithful, appointing me to the ministry—even though I was formerly a blasphemer, a persecutor, and an arrogant man. But I received mercy because I acted out of ignorance in unbelief, and the grace of our Lord overflowed, along with the faith and love that are in Christ Jesus. This saying is trustworthy and deserving of full acceptance: "Christ Jesus came into the world to save sinners"—and I am the worst of them. But I received mercy for this reason, so that in me, the worst of them, Christ Jesus might demonstrate his extraordinary patience as an example to those who would believe in him for eternal life.

> If God's work through us isn't limited by what we've done in the past, how would you verbalize the way God intends to work through us?

> If God can use us no matter where we've been or what we've done, what does that capability say about taking pride in our accomplishments?

EXPRESS

"My concern is that older church leaders aren't doing enough to pass the faith to the next generation. I sometimes wonder if young-adult Christians feel as if they're reaching back and nothing is there. Intergenerational mentoring can correct that problem" (p. 50).

> Recall the communities of faith you've been a part of. In those experiences was faith being passed to a new generation?

> What elements of faith do you consider essential for the next generation to understand?

Watch video session 3, "Dave, Teddy, and Patrick's Story."

> What stands out to you from Dave's, Teddy's, and Patrick's comments about their mentoring relationships?

In the video Dave makes the following statement: "I believe as believers in Christ that we should be constantly seeking the counsel of those who've been doing it longer than we have. But I also believe that we should be pouring our lives into those who haven't been doing it as long as we have. It just makes a lot of sense to be able to learn from each other."

> What are some benefits of this dual approach to mentoring we've discussed? What are some the hurdles?

> How does the focus on being mentored and mentoring at the same time help ensure that faith is being passed to the next generation?

EQUIP

Pray in pairs. Ask each pair to identify the names of mentors who taught them something about faith. Then have them offer prayers of thanks for those people by name. Next lead them to pray for each other—that they'll have a faith worth passing to the next generation.

SESSION 4
Taking the First Steps

ENGAGE

"One of the most common problems in mentoring relationships, as in other ongoing relationships, is unmet expectations. Discussing expectations at the start can protect the relationship from hurt feelings and awkwardness later" (p. 65).

> What makes it difficult to talk about expectations as you begin any relationship?

> Think about a relationship you've been disappointed in. How did your disappointment relate to your expectations for that relationship?

> If you were a mentor, what you would want a mentee to expect from you?

ENCOUNTER

"Mentoring is about reproduction. Multiplication. Growing influence. Making disciples. It's about finding someone like Paul in your life, someone to learn from, so that you in turn can teach a Timothy, someone who can learn from you" (p. 68).

> How would you compare this description of mentoring with your observations and experiences in churches or other faith communities?

> What do you see as the value of having a variety of different mentors, some more intensive than others?

> **Read Ephesians 4:15-16.**
> *Speaking the truth in love, let us grow in every way into him who is the head—Christ. From him the whole body, fitted and knit together by every supporting ligament, promotes the growth of the body for building up itself in love by the proper working of each individual part.*

> What kind of spiritual growth do you think happens best in community or at least in a relationship, rather than in solitude?

> Think about the faith communities you've been a part of, formally or informally. How did you perceive that your individual spiritual growth (or lack of it) affected the whole group?

> **Read 1 Corinthians 12:22-25.**
> *Those parts of the body that are weaker are indispensable. And those parts of the body that we consider less honorable, we clothe these with greater honor, and our unrespectable parts are treated with greater respect, which our respectable parts do not need. Instead, God has put the body together, giving greater honor to the less honorable, so that there would be no division† in the body, but that the members would have the same concern for each other.*

> What members of a faith community would you consider to be the weaker members?

> List a variety of ways the strong members of a church body can help the weak.

EXPRESS

"God divinely intersects your life with the lives of your mentor and mentee. He uses each of you to urge the others toward Christlikeness. Meanwhile, the enemy stands ready to oppose. We must pray for one another. Pray for yourself. Pray for your Paul. Pray for your Timothy" (p. 70).

> How would you describe the balance between depending on a mentor and ultimately trusting God with your spiritual growth?

> Which do you think would be more difficult—to make a request to be mentored or to mentor someone? Compare the challenges of both.

   Watch video session 4, "Carrie and Courtney's Story."

> What stands out to you from Carrie's and Courtney's comments about their mentoring relationship.

> Which of the five action steps discussed in this session are evident in Carrie and Courtney's story?

EQUIP

Ask group members to mentally envision their next year: goals they have, events they'll go to, trips they'll take, job changes they'll experience, purchases they'll make, and milestones they'll experience. Then ask them to pray for the people God will bring into their lives as their mentors—that group members will recognize these people and will listen to what they have to say. Then have members pray for the people God will bring into their lives as their mentees—that they will recognize those people and will know how to influence them. Close by praying for the group and all that God will accomplish through their lives during the next year.

SESSION 5
Developing a Plan of Action

ENGAGE
"Much of mentoring involves challenging people to do something—to take steps toward growth. The responsibilities of mentors are to guide their mentees, support them in their tasks, and encourage them toward progress in the Christian life" (p. 83).

Watch video session 5, "Arliss and Linda's Story."

> What stands out to you from Arliss's and Linda's comments about their mentoring relationship?

> What do both Arliss and Linda reveal about their commitment to the spiritual journeys and growth processes of the people in their lives?

> If a mentee is already motivated to grow in an area, describe why he or she could still benefit from a mentor.

> Given that the purpose of mentoring is to help another person change, how would you differentiate it from instruction?

ENCOUNTER
"God outfits us for the spiritual battle we're engaged in, but knowing how to use that gear requires training. ... Keep in mind that [God's armor isn't] separate pieces. It's all connected around God's Word. Also remember that training to wear and use God's armor is more than simply teaching a lesson. Effective mentoring requires sharing life. As mentors and mentees walk together, they learn to wear the armor of God every day" (p. 76).

> What spiritual tools have you used most often in your spiritual journey?

> Recount one of your earliest memories of seeing someone become an example to you by the way he or she walked in faith.

Read Ephesians 6:10-18.
Be strengthened by the Lord and by his vast strength. Put on the full armor of God so that you can stand against the schemes of the devil. For our struggle is not against flesh and blood, but against the rulers, against the authorities, against the cosmic powers of this darkness, against evil, spiritual forces in the heavens. For this reason take up the full armor of God, so that you may be able to resist in the evil day, and having prepared everything, to take your stand. Stand, therefore, with truth like a belt around your waist, righteousness like armor on your chest, and your feet sandaled with readiness for the gospel of peace. In every situation take up the shield of faith with which you can extinguish all the flaming arrows of the evil one. Take the helmet of salvation and the sword of the Spirit—which is the word of God. Pray at all times in the Spirit with every prayer and request, and stay alert with all perseverance and intercession for all the saints.

> Which of these pieces of armor bring to your mind situations you've faced that required spiritual equipment?

> In what ways have you used prayer as a spiritual tool?

> Which part of God's armor is the most difficult for you to use well and consistently?

> **Read 1 Peter 5:6-9.**
> *Humble yourselves, therefore, under the mighty hand of God, so that he may exalt you at the proper time, casting all your cares on him, because he cares about you. Be sober-minded, be alert. Your adversary the devil is prowling around like a roaring lion, looking for anyone he can devour. Resist him, firm in the faith, knowing that the same kind of sufferings are being experienced by your fellow believers throughout the world.*

> Living a life of faith requires both cooperating with the Spirit of God and resisting Satan. In what ways does being in a mentoring relationship help with both sides of that equation?

EXPRESS

"In mentoring relationships we hold each other accountable to God's Word, push for holiness, and pick up each other when we fall. This is one area where mentors must be especially willing to be vulnerable" (p. 77).

> When someone spiritually trips and falls, why do we sometimes feel awkward in approaching that person?

> What do you want and need from your siblings in Christ after you've spiritually fallen?

EQUIP

Take prayer requests for individuals group members know who are struggling with their faith. Write those names in a place where the group can see them. Then divide into small groups to pray. Ask the groups to pray for the people whose names are listed and for one another, particularly that they'll maintain strong faith and steadfast resistance to the enemy.

SESSION 6
Preparing for Potholes and Possibilities

ENGAGE
"I don't know what journey God has planned for your life. … But I know He expects someone to help you grow in your Christian faith. He wants other believers to disciple you, to walk with you along the way as you become more Christlike" (p. 102).

> Of the two roles—mentoring and being mentored—which holds the greatest challenges (the most potential potholes) for you?

> After all you've considered during this study, how would you state in your own words the value of mentors in the body of Christ?

> **Watch video session 6, "Jason and Dakota's Story."**

> What stands out to you from Jason's and Dakota's comments about their mentoring relationship?

> Of the possibilities of mentoring discussed in session 6, which is Jason currently putting into practice as he invests in Dakota's life?

ENCOUNTER
"The final stage of effective mentoring results in a new mentor/mentee relationship as the mentee becomes the mentor. The first-generation mentoring relationship really isn't complete until a second-generation relationship is established" (p. 96).

> Think about the potholes mentioned in this session: failing to establish expectations, tutoring rather than mentoring, refusing to confront, developing jealousy, surrendering to spiritual letdown, and choosing not to multiply. Which do you consider the most troublesome from your experience?

> Besides the potential potholes mentioned in this session, what are some other reasons a person who's been mentored might not choose to mentor someone else?

> We've read about different kinds of mentors—occasional, informal, intensive. How are these styles of mentoring different from the mentoring you've experienced? What are their advantages?

> **Read James 5:16.**
> *Confess your sins to one another and pray for one another, so that you may be healed. The prayer of a righteous person is very powerful in its effect.*

> One pothole mentioned in this session is spiritual letdown, the process by which we give each other unspoken permission to live below the biblical standard we profess to live by. How can this pothole be addressed by the confession mentioned in James 5:16? How can we confess our sins to each other honestly and hold each other accountable without feeling either judged or excused? How should that dynamic work in a mentoring relationship?

Read 2 Timothy 3:14-17.

Continue in what you have learned and firmly believed. You know those who taught you, and you know that from infancy you have known the sacred Scriptures, which are able to give you wisdom for salvation through faith in Christ Jesus. All Scripture is inspired by God and is profitable for teaching, for rebuking, for correcting, for training in righteousness, so that the man of God may be complete, equipped for every good work.

> How would you describe the role Scripture plays in Christian mentoring?

Read Philippians 1:3-8.

I give thanks to my God for every remembrance of you, always praying with joy for all of you in my every prayer, because of your partnership in the gospel from the first day until now. I am sure of this, that he who started a good work in you will carry it on to completion until the day of Christ Jesus. Indeed, it is right for me to think this way about all of you, because I have you in my heart, and you are all partners with me in grace, both in my imprisonment and in the defense and confirmation of the gospel. For God is my witness, how deeply I miss all of you with the affection of Christ Jesus.

> These verses from Paul and Timothy, though written to a group rather than an individual, portray the close bond that can develop in a mentoring relationship. What portion of these verses most accurately describes your greatest hope for the people you mentor?

> Think about the benefits of mentoring mentioned in this session: finding authentic, rich relationships; expanding your influence; appreciating and offering grace; and receiving blessings and prayers. Which of these potential outcomes would hold the greatest benefit for you?

EXPRESS

"Somebody is waiting to disciple you along the way. Be patient but persistent as you pray to find this person. Then go, walk in his or her shadow, and discover the power of God. Finally, in that power invest yourself in someone else" (p. 102).

> How do you think your life would benefit from pursuing a mentoring relationship?

> How do you look at mentoring differently now, compared to when you began this study?

EQUIP

To close your final group time, ask the group to stand and huddle together closely. Pray over them, closing your prayer with 2 Timothy 2:1-2:

You, therefore, my son, be strong in the grace that is in Christ Jesus. What you have heard from me in the presence of many witnesses, commit to faithful men who will be able to teach others also.

Ask for God's blessing and guidance as you seek to learn from others and pass on the lessons of discipleship you've learned.

MORE BIBLE STUDIES

CREATION UNRAVELED
THE GOSPEL ACCORDING TO GENESIS
BY MATT CARTER AND HALIM SUH

The words we read in Genesis are the same words that provided hope for hungry Israelites in the wilderness, breathed courage into the heart of David, and fed the soul of Jesus Himself during His time on earth. God's promises are as relevant today as they were "in the beginning."

CREATION RESTORED
THE GOSPEL ACCORDING TO GENESIS
BY MATT CARTER AND HALIM SUH

Examine Genesis 12–50 and explore how the early portions of the Bible foreshadow the gospel of Jesus Christ—the good news of salvation and redemption that we find only in relationship with Him. When we read about Abraham, Jacob, and Joseph—the family of promise—we read about salvation by faith. We begin to understand that God orchestrates everything, including suffering and evil, in order to redeem the consequences of the fall and ultimately restore us to Him.

SAMSON
A LIFE WELL WASTED
BY CHIP HENDERSON

Samson was uniquely dedicated to God, and he experienced the power of God's Spirit. Yet he failed to embrace his God-given purpose, and his unfaithfulness to God led to his destruction and death. This study examines the major flaws in Samson's life, showing how easily we can waste our lives when we fail to accept God's purpose for us. Learn how you can avoid major pitfalls and embrace what God has created you for.

ENGAGE
A PRACTICAL GUIDE TO EVANGELISM
BY J. D. GREEAR, ROB TURNER, DERWIN GRAY, AND BEN REED

The simple truth of the gospel doesn't change. And while this truth is timeless, we must always evaluate the presentation of that truth to make sure it's connecting in a culturally relevant way. This practical study examines the act of sharing your faith. It answers questions like: How do you begin a conversation about Jesus? What if people have questions you're not sure how to answer? What do you say if they respond positively or if they reject God's message?

ORDINARY
HOW TO TURN THE WORLD UPSIDE DOWN
BY TONY MERIDA

The kingdom of God isn't coming with light shows and shock and awe but with lowly acts of service performed in the normal rhythms of life. *Ordinary* encourages participants to move into a life of mission and justice—speaking up for the voiceless, caring for the single mom, restoring the broken, bearing burdens, welcoming the functionally fatherless, and speaking the good news to people on a regular basis in order to change the world..

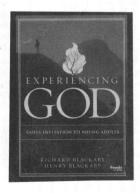

EXPERIENCING GOD
GOD'S INVITATION TO YOUNG ADULTS
BY HENRY T. BLACKABY AND RICHARD BLACKABY

What should I do with my life? How can God use me? Many of us ask those questions, but none more so than young adults. If you're searching for God's will and practical advice as you seek answers to important life decisions, *Experiencing God: God's Invitation to Young Adults* is for you. The goal of this Bible study is to teach you how to live your life in such a way that you'll experience everything God intends for your life. This will happen when you fully embrace God's invitation to live through Him.

GROUP CONTACT INFORMATION

Name _____ Number _____

Email _____

Name _____ Number _____

Email _____

Name _____ Number _____

Email _____

Name _____ Number _____

Email _____

Name _____ Number _____

Email _____

Name _____ Number _____

Email _____

Name _____ Number _____

Email _____

Name _____ Number _____

Email _____

Name _____ Number _____

Email _____

Name _____ Number _____

Email _____

Name _____ Number _____

Email _____